4

Ingredients

FAST, FRESH & HEALTHY

HAY
HOUSE

HAY HOUSE, INC.
Carlsbad, California • New York City
London • Sydney • Johannesburg
Vancouver • Hong Kong • New Delhi

Published and Distributed in Australia and New Zealand by:
Hay House Australia Pty. Ltd. - www.hayhouse.com.au

ISBN: 9781401924348

13 12 11 10   5 4 3 2 1
1st edition, August 2010

Cover Design & Typesetting: Allure Creative
Printed in Australia by: McPherson's Printing Group

4 Ingredients
PO Box 1171, Mooloolaba QLD 4557
www.4ingredients.com.au • info@4ingredients.com.au
ABN: 19 307 118 068

Preface

Since the release of our first book, we have been constantly asked to bring out a recipe book that focuses on a healthier lifestyle. As everyone knows, our forte is making meals simple and easy to prepare. So when the opportunity came up to work with the foremost authority on mind-body medicine in the world Deepak Chopra, we believed that this was perfect timing. Through our collaboration, we believe we have come up with the best of all worlds when it comes to delivering healthy and simple meals.

For those of you who have not been exposed to Ayurvedic principles, it's a tried and true ancient system that is followed by millions of individuals around the world. Ayurveda, in Sanskrit, means "the science of life." It is a philosophy that's been around for at least 4,000 years, focusing on prevention, healing and wellbeing. Balance is very important in Ayurveda and strives to harmonise through the combination of diet, meditation, massage, essential oils and herbs.

The pure Ayurvedic principles that Deepak and many others follow are much deeper and more precise than what we have presented in this book. It was Deepak's intention only to touch on the principles and offer some guidelines by way of an introduction to what is possible. The recipes may not follow the strictest Ayurvedic requirements, but that wasn't the purpose of this book. Our intention is to introduce the concepts of what has worked so well in the East, in the hope that our readers can apply them to their very busy and demanding lifestyles. We wish to encourage everyone to explore all forms of a healthy and holistic lifestyle so that healthy, and simple choices become the obvious ones to make...

See you on the journey!

Kim & Rachael

Thank you

We are continually *amazed* at how the journey of *4 Ingredients* has grown from two mums who had a desire to write a cookbook, to help save time and money and put great food on the table for our families, to the global enterprise it has grown into in just a few years.

Of course this did not happen without *LOTS* of time and energy and without some special people in our lives.

We would like to thank Leon Nacson from Hay House for approaching us with the possibility of working with Deepak Chopra and then making this book happen.

Thanks so much to our incredibly supportive husbands who are still happily taste testing all our delicious 4 ingredient recipes and minding our beautiful children. We could *NEVER* do what we do without both of you!

To our gorgeous family and friends who have helped us research, compile, shop, cook , clean and taste-test hundreds of recipes for this book. There are many of you but we'd like to pay special thanks to Jennette McCosker, Spud Moore, Jules Boag, Wendy Beattie, Michelle Tuite, Jeff Thode, Angela Covino and Dan Primmer— this book is what it has become because you all sprinkled your magic within its pages somewhere.

To our beautiful team who help us keep the balance; Mel Davis, Leona Bowles, Melinda Dines and Danae McAulay for often going above and beyond the call of duty to help make our lives *MUCH* easier—thanks girls!

Thank you to all of you who have sent us recipes, we delight in receiving every single one of them. Food is the ultimate universal language; we all have to eat and it's exciting receiveing recipes from all over the world. So please, keep them coming, we will experiment with all of them.

And finally, to all of you for buying our cookbooks to use yourselves or as gifts for others, we know you'll absolutely *LOOOOVE* this book. Not only will it enable you to get delicious recipes on the table for you and your family, it will also help you save time and money in the kitchen and hopefully be your mind and body's new best friend!

Happy Cooking!

Rachael & Kim

In the Cupboard

4 Ingredients offers a wide range of yummy recipes, cooked for our families and friends for many a BBQ, party, Sunday dinner, Friday drinks and so on. In all our trials and errors there seemed to be a bunch of staple ingredients we always called upon. What we aim to do in this section is help you stock your kitchen pantry with those basic ingredients that will help flavour, make and save many a dish and event from peril.

Please note: In this book we have not included salt, pepper and water as part of the 4 Ingredients.

SAVOURY	SWEET
Sea salt	Plain flour
Peppercorns	Organic self raising flour
Vinegar	Rapadura or raw sugar
Lemons	Icing sugar
Soy sauce	Food colouring
Fresh garlic	Vanilla essence
Sesame oil & seeds	Condensed milk
Minced ginger	Cream cheese
Sweet-chilli sauce	Puff pastry
Whole-egg mayonnaise	Mixed fruit
Garlic	Jams; apricot, strawberry
Basil Pesto	Arrowroot biscuits
Cold pressed extra virgin macadamia oil	Honey
Extra virgin macadamia oil spray	Caster sugar
Bread crumbs	Evaporated milk
Sour cream	Mixed spices
French onion soup (dry mix)	Cinnamon
Dijon mustard	Nutmeg
Wholegrain mustard	Cornflour
Spaghetti & Noodles	Eggs
Brown rice	Marmalade
Jasmine rice	Gelatine
Sesame seeds	Tin of crushed pineapple
Pine nuts	Jelly crystals
Organic organic tomato sauce	Packet of bamboo skewers
BBQ sauce	
Worcestershire sauce	
Beef and chicken stock cubes	

Guide to Weights & Measures

A complex conversion table is not required as all you need to make the recipes within each edition of *4 Ingredients* are:

1 Teaspoon	=	1 tsp.
1 Tablespoon	=	1 tbs.
1 Cup	=	250ml or the following:

Gram Weights & Equivalents

Product	Grams Per Cup	Product	Grams Per Cup
Almond Meal	170	Nuts – Pecans	120
Butter	230	Nuts – Almonds	160
Bail Pesto	260	Nuts – Pistachios	120
Breadcrumbs	130	Pasta (dried)	75
Brown sugar, packed	220	Peanut butter	260
Caster sugar	200	Popcorn	40
Cheese	100	Raisins	170
Chutney	300	Rice	185
Cornflakes	120	Rice bubbles	80
Cornflour	120	Rolled oats	100
Desiccated Coconut	120	Salsa	175
Dried apricots	160	Self raising flour	175
Dried mixed fruit	170	Sour cream	320
Flour	175	Sultanas	170
Honey	320	Sugar – White	220
Icing Sugar	120	Sugar – Raw	200
Jam	320	Tandoori paste	225
Mayonnaise	260	Tomato paste	260
Natural Muesli	110	Yoghurt	250

Abbreviations Used

Gram	g
Kilogram	kg
Millilitre	ml
Litre	ltr

Oven Temperature Guide

Making friends with your oven really helps when cooking. Basically, the Celsius temperature is about half the Fahrenheit temperature.

A lot of ovens these days offer the option to bake or fan bake (amongst others), as a rule, having the fan assisted option on will greatly increase the temperature in your oven and will shorten cooking times.

Our recipes have been compiled assuming a static conventional oven (non fan-forced) unless otherwise stated. If, however, your oven is fan forced, as a general rule of thumb, reduce the temperature by 20°C (this may vary between models). So if the recipe reads bake for 1 hour at 200°C that will be 1 hour at 180°C fan-forced.

Here's some help:

	Slow	Slow	Mod	Mod	Mod hot	Mod hot	Hot	Hot	Very hot
Fahrenheit	275	300	325	350	375	400	425	450	475
Celsius	140	150	165	180	190	200	220	230	240
Gas Mark	1	2	3	4	5	6	7	8	9

Healthy Food Substitutes

What we would really have loved is to have substituted many of our everyday household products for healthier alternatives. The main reason being is that natural, non-technically enhanced products are LOADED with essential nutrients that fuel your body, mind and soul. Apart from the obvious short and long term benefits of consuming these ingredients, you can literally taste the difference.

However not wanting to isolate those that are not able to purchase these products readily, we did not include these within our recipes, opting instead to add this section, which we feel, is vital to your and your families' health. For those of you able to access these products readily, the table below will show you what mainstream ingredient can be easily substituted with a healthier (and less technically altered and therefore nutrient drained) alternative. For more information on this we recommend our good friend Cyndi O'Meara's book, *Changing Habits Changing Lives*:

PRODUCT	SUBSTITUTE
Sugar	• Organic raw sugar*
Oil	• Cold pressed extra virgin olive oil* • Cold pressed macadamia nut oil* • Sunflower, rice bran, walnut oils
Spray Oil	• Cold pressed macadamia nut oil * (or if you can't find, use one of the above oils in your own spray bottle)
Flour	• Spelt flour • Organic plain flour and Organic baking powder* • Organic self raising flour
Margarine	• Butter*
Eggs	• Organic free range eggs*
Milk	• Organic milk* • Raw milk • Pasteurised only milk
Pasta	• Made from fresh ingredients • Organic Pasta*
Honey	• Manuka honey* • Organic honey*
Jams	• Organic jam* • Homemade jams made from raw ingredients
Soy Sauce	• Tamari soy sauce*

*Note — all ingredients with an asterisk * can now be bought in your local supermarket. Where possible buy products labeled 'certified organic' as these products have passed all the stringent tests to ensure that they really are organic and therefore are loaded with nutrients and flavour.*

The Basic Ingredients for a Healthier Mind & Body

by Deepak Chopra

If you understand just these four basic ingredients for healthy living you will be well on your way to a healthier mind and body.

1. *There is a genius inside you and me*. Our bodies have an *inner intelligence*. In other words, our bodies know exactly what it is we need to eat (and when) for us to be healthy. Just as your brain takes in certain pieces of information and works out what to do with them, your digestive system takes in the food you eat and works out what it can use, what it will get rid of and what it will store.

2. *Your cells recreate themselves over and over* millions of times in your lifetime. We are being created anew each day. The skin, for example, replaces itself once each month, the stomach lining every five days, the liver every six weeks, and the skeleton every three months. In fact, each year around 98 per cent of each one of us is made up of brand new cells. So, even if you are feeling overweight or unhealthy today, there is no reason that you have to stay that way.

3. *There is a mind/body connection*. In recent times science is confirming more and more what some cultures have known for thousands of years: your thoughts and feelings can have a direct affect on your body's organs and cells, so it makes sense to keep a positive attitude around eating and exercise.

4. *Everything you eat has an effect on your body*. There are many books and research papers to prove this, but we've promised to keep this book really simple. So for now, let's just say that YOU BECOME WHAT YOU EAT.

This book is a back-to-basics approach to food preparation designed to guide you on your path to creating better health EASILY. If you are after an instant weight loss program you won't find it in these pages. When you really pay attention to your appetite your body finds its own natural weight, whatever this may be. And just for the record...

Food is more than just protein, carbohydrate and fat.

Your relationship with food needs to provide you with a sense of joy, growth and enrichment. You don't need to count calories, kilojoules or grams of fat; you need to simply develop more of an *awareness* around the food, you are choosing to eat day to day. When you pay attention to what your body wants to eat and when it wants to eat, you will experience positive change.

Healthy food was designed over millions of years to be pleasurable.

Food doesn't have to be bland to be healthy. The flavours of life in the right proportion add richness to our food and our experience. Your body will respond well if you spice up the food you eat. If you are not enjoying your food the nutritional, emotional, psychological and physical benefits of a meal will be greatly reduced.

Kim and Rachael have created recipes and food preparation ideas that incorporate wonderful colours, stimulating aromas and a variety of flavours, textures and spices to completely satisfy your taste buds. The recipes are simple, healthy and environmentally sustainable.

I personally follow the Ayurvedic tradition which avoids pork and beef in particular, however this is a personal choice. These recipes provide health options for *all* tastes and are designed to excite your senses, to invigorate your taste buds and of course, to completely satisfy your appetite.

By becoming aware of the way you currently behave towards food, you will be able to make changes for the better. When you change your way of eating by changing a few simple rules, you will create a healthier, more vital body that is capable of providing you with more strength, joy and pleasure!

Healthy Eating Can Be Easy

Eating is one of the most natural processes in the world and it can be quite easy and enjoyable to follow a healthy diet. So why are so many people confused about what is good for them to eat?

As our world becomes 'smaller' we are given so many choices. We have access to grains, nuts and fruits from across the other side of the world, we can choose from full-cream, low-fat, no-fat, lite, skim, biodynamic, organic, high-calcium, low dairy *and* soy milks, and are bombarded with a wide range of dietary powders, pills and potions that promise instant weight reduction.

One day we are told by the 'experts' that chocolate and coffee are bad for us, the next day we're told they are good for us. We are told to eat more protein and fewer carbohydrates, and then told this is not healthy. We're told that low-fat diets are better for us, and then we are told by someone else that this is incorrect. For every diet, nutritional plan or exercise machine that is presented that 'really works' there is someone who will tell us why it doesn't.

This situation has come about because over the years people have stopped paying attention to their own stomach; they've lost what is known as *'the mind/body connection'* (being in tune with what the body really wants and needs). When we were children, many of us were taught to eat when it was *'time'* to eat and to eat everything on our plate whether we were hungry or not. The current high levels of obesity around the world are not surprising considering how many children are encouraged to disregard the signals from their own body.

It's time for us to re-engage this 'mind/body connection' and make healthier eating an easy and joyful experience.

Healthy eating = healthy weight.

The basic information and simple food preparation tips in this book will help you to get back to basics. Before we do that, let's take a quick look at a different understanding of healthy living from another culture.

What is Ayurveda?

To maintain my own good health I follow Ayurvedic principles. Ayurveda (pronounced ah-your-vay-duuh) is a traditional Indian science of health that is over 5000 years old. The word can be translated as 'the wisdom of life' or 'the science of longevity'.

Ayurveda offers an approach to living that is based on a very important principle: it says body, mind and soul are completely dependent on one another, and slowly, science is coming to the same conclusion.

4 Golden Rules of Healthy Eating

If you follow these four golden rules every day you will experience a total change in your well being and enjoy a healthier weight.

1. Pay attention to your appetite and only eat when you are truly hungry.

2. Sample each of Ayurveda's 6 Essential Tastes of Life every day, eating fresh, delicious, healthy foods that you enjoy.

3. Choose food that nourishes your body and emotions.

4. Eat with awareness.

Apply these principles until they become your natural way of eating. Read these four golden rules every morning as a reminder of the new way you are going to approach your eating habits. Let's look at each one in more detail.

1. Pay attention to your appetite and only eat when you are truly hungry.

Your appetite is your friend, don't think of it as the enemy. A strong appetite is one of the most important signs of good health, it can tell you what to eat and when so you can feel healthier and happier. Don't make your appetite 'wrong' and try to fight it—you will be fighting against your own body's messages about what it needs. Instead, be thankful for your body's wonderful ability to tell you what it needs through your appetite.

Most people eat out of habit, to be social, because they are stressed or lonely, or because someone tells them that it's time to eat.

Hunger is a signal from your body that it wants to eat and is ready to metabolise food properly (this means it will use the nutrients it needs and get rid of the rest easily). If you're not hungry, your body doesn't need anything at that time, and more importantly, the body hasn't prepared itself properly to be able to digest what you do eat.

Next time you go to eat something, place your hand on your stomach and check in—are you actually feeling hungry? If not, don't eat! You might like to drink a glass of water instead.

If you are hungry, only eat until you start to feel satisfied—and not a bit more! Avoid eating to the point of heaviness, dullness or discomfort (how you might feel after trying everything at a large buffet or smorgasbord).

The other side of this is that it is important never to let yourself feel starved, because the body's 'intelligence' might think that means there won't be any food for a while and it could reset its metabolism (the speed at which it uses up or stores food) to protect against starvation by storing the food you eat. The less you eat, the slower your metabolism can get and the more weight you can gain! Eating healthy food only when you are hungry can help your body to maintain an efficient metabolism.

Here's a simple exercise to help you to break out of old eating patterns:

EAT whenever you're HUNGRY,
but when you're NOT hungry, DON'T EAT.

Doing this for two weeks will give you time to become more aware of your body's signals.

If possible, **eat your heaviest meal at lunch time** because digestion is stronger at midday and is more efficient at converting food into energy instead of into fat. After a while you'll find that you won't even feel like a heavy meal at dinner—a time when digestion isn't at its strongest. Don't be too hard on yourself if you do find yourself out to dinner in the evening. Just check your appetite and eat something delicious in small portions until you begin to feel satisfied but not uncomfortable.

This approach to eating is not dieting, it's simply paying attention to your body and its level of genuine satisfaction.

2. Sample each of the 6 Essential Tastes of Life every day, eating fresh, delicious, healthy foods that you enjoy.

Remember, healthy food doesn't have to be bland—far from it. Nature can provide all our dietary needs when eaten in the correct way at the correct time.

In Ayurveda all foods are placed into six categories according to their taste and the effect they have on the body. We need a wide variety of foods in our daily diet. Rather than fretting over charts, counting grams of fat and feeling guilty about cravings, you can make sure you are getting all the health benefits food offers by including each of the 6 Essential Tastes in your daily meals. Also, having a diet balanced in all six tastes is extremely helpful in satisfying food cravings.

The 6 Essential Tastes of Life: sweet, sour, salty, pungent, bitter, stringent.

Sweet

Most carbohydrates are considered to be part of this 'sweet' family. Most sweet foods are high in fibre, but of course we know that eating lots of refined sugar and starch (which also tastes sweet) isn't healthy for us. It's important for you to eat something from the sweet family each day, and if you choose the *healthy* options, over time your body won't crave sweets in a form that is not healthy (such as processed cakes, pastries and fast foods).

Sweet foods: *sugar, honey, wholegrain rice, pasta, milk, cream, butter, whole grains, cereals. Fresh fruit such as mangoes, melons, bananas, peaches; crunchy nuts. Fresh vegetables such as corn and avocado.*

Consider reducing cholesterol-rich foods and avoid foods containing hydrogenated oils. *Meat* is also considered part of the 'sweet' family. Consider reducing the amount of meat that you eat to two meals per week, or replacing red meat with cold-water (oily) *fish* or *free range* chicken and *turkey*.

Sour

Oranges, lemons, pineapples, plums, blueberries, raspberries, strawberries, yoghurt and *tomatoes* all belong to the 'sour' family, as does *cheese* and *vinegar*. Their slightly sour taste adds a little acidic flavour to your meals. They can also bring wonderful health benefits, so be sure to experience this taste each day. Cut down on pickled foods, green olives, alcohol and vinegar.

Salty

In the right doses, salt adds flavour and stimulates digestion, but you need to choose the salt you use carefully and use it sparingly for best benefits, especially if you experience high blood pressure or fluid retention. Be aware that salt is also found in soy sauce, many tinned and processed foods and salted meats. There are many *organic salts* that are full of flavour and minerals, and *seaweed* is a tasty, natural form of salt.

Pungent

Think of the kick of *pepper*, the bite of *chilli*, the tang of *ginger* and the heat-producing effects they all have—these are 'pungent' foods. These flavours help digestion and have been known to stimulate metabolism. *Garlic* and *onions* have been shown to help lower cholesterol and blood pressure. The delicious smells and flavours offered by pungent foods add a delightful touch to every meal.

Pungent foods include *peppers (cayenne, black and chilli), fresh and dry ginger, horseradish, onions, garlic, leeks, mustard, cloves, cinnamon, peppermint, thyme, cumin, cardamom, basil, oregano* and *rosemary*.

Bitter

Members of the 'bitter' family include dark green and yellow vegetables such as *broccoli, kale, spinach, cauliflower, endive, chicory, asparagus* and *lettuce*—all are foods rich in nutrients that have been known to fight infections and have been useful for detoxifying and strengthening the immune system.

Astringent

Think of the slightly tart taste of a fresh green apple and you can imagine the 'astringent' family. *Cranberries, beans, lentils, peas, cabbage, pomegranates, pears* and *green tea* are astringent, as are the purple and red vegetables such as *eggplant*. Astringent foods provide a contrast to the sweet family, keep your taste buds clear and sensitive, and have been known to assist in cell renewal.

6 Essential Tastes Chart

You may need a little help to change your eating habits to include the 6 Essential Tastes every day. Place a copy of this chart in a convenient place in the kitchen and carry one with you when you shop for groceries to help remind you of the foods you're wanting to include in your diet.

It's important that you don't make choosing what to eat hard work. Don't worry if you get to the end of the day and realise you've missed out on one or more of the tastes—this will be a long-term lifestyle change that you'll balance out over time. You will feel so much better when you incorporate the 6 Essential Tastes that you'll find it easy and fun to adjust your diet to include them.

SWEET		SOUR	
Milk	Honey	Limes	
Butter	Raw Sugar	Lemon	
Cream	Ripe Fresh Fruit	Citrus Fruit	
Wheat	Rolled Oats	Yoghurt	
Ghee	Raw Sugar	Mango Powder	
Rice	Raisins	Many Immature Fruits	
Maple Syrup	Cranberries	Tamarind	
Sesame Oil	Honey	Plums	
Apple Juice	Soy Milk	Blueberries	
Coconut Milk	Vanilla Extract	Raspberries	
SALTY		**BITTER**	
Salt	Tamari Soy Sauce	Greens	Turmeric
Pickles	Seaweed	• Kale	Fenugreek
Salty Pretzels		• Broccoli	Endive
		• Spinach	Chicory
		• Lettuce	
PUNGENT (generally hot & spicy)		**ASTRINGENT** (a dry & light taste)	
Chilli Pepper	Salsa	Apples	Green Tea
Ginger	Onions	Apricots	Lentils
Black Pepper	Asparagus	Beans	Peaches
Clove	Spinach	Berries	Persimmons
Mustard	Tomatoes	Cabbage	Pomegranates
Radish	Fresh chillies	Cauliflower	Prunes
Daikon	Garlic	Cherries	Raisins
Onions	Cinnamon	Coriander	Strawberries
Thyme	Basil	Figs (dry)	Turmeric
Oregano	Rosemary	Grapes	

There are foods that taste delicious to us, and other foods that don't. There is enough variety in the 6 Essential Tastes for you to choose a daily eating program that will not only taste good, but also be good for you—and you won't need to feel as if you're missing out! You will always feel satisfied and you will begin to crave healthy food that makes you feel good when you eat it.

3. Choose food that nourishes your body and emotions.

Fresh is always best for your body, as fresh food is full of nutrients and energy. You've seen the difference between a lettuce picked fresh out of the garden and one that has been sitting in the bottom of your fridge for two weeks. Frozen, canned, processed, reheated and leftover foods have much much less 'life' than fresh food—and organic food is free of chemicals.

As you begin to appreciate the food you put into your body you might even feel inspired to grow your own vegetables, herbs and fruits!

Satisfying cravings

Giving in to unhealthy cravings can sabotage your efforts. If you experience cravings, it's usually for sweet foods. This shouldn't be ignored. By making healthy choices from the 'sweet' family you can satisfy those cravings with more wholesome, healthy foods such as sweet fruits, whole grains and nuts.

While incorporating the 6 Essential Tastes into your daily diet is a long-term healthy life choice, there are some foods that can particularly help you to be a healthy weight. Choose...

- Foods that are light, dry and warm; spicy, bitter and astringent (see the 6 Essential Tastes chart).

- Lighter fruits such as apples, pears, pomegranates, cranberries and persimmons.

- Honey is excellent (never heat honey).

- All beans.

- Light grains such as barley, corn, millet, buckwheat and rye.

- All spices except salt.

- All vegetables, especially radishes, asparagus, eggplant, green leafy vegetables, beets, broccoli, potatoes, cabbage, carrots, cauliflower, pumpkin, lettuce, celery and sprouts.

- If you do eat meat, choose cold-water (oily) fish and white meat such as free-range chicken and turkey.

4. Eat with awareness.

In this fast-paced world you may often feel that you just don't have the time to pay attention to your diet, but eating with awareness is vital to your body's ability to digest the foods you eat. This doesn't mean being a slave to meal times, but here are some tips that will help your body to digest the food you eat more easily.

- Eat in a calm and quiet atmosphere. How we are feeling when we eat can affect how well we digest it. Your attention should be on the food, not divided between eating and watching television, reading, etc. And don't eat when you are upset or angry; postpone the meal for a few minutes until you feel more settled.

- Always sit down to eat, even if it is just a snack. Taking the time to pay attention to what you are doing will help to prepare your digestion and allow you time to check in on your true hunger level.

- Avoid ice cold foods and drinks as they tend to freeze the digestive 'fires' that you need to help with the healthy breakdown of foods. It may take a little time to break the habit, but you'll find after time you won't miss cold drinks.

- Don't talk while chewing—focus inward, enjoying the taste, sight and smell of the food you are eating.

- Eat slowly to give your body a chance to digest food properly. Put your fork or spoon down in between mouthfuls to help you to slow down and don't take another mouthful until the last one has been chewed and swallowed.

- Sit quietly for a few minutes after your meal to allow digestion to begin.

Beware of quick fixes

Many people struggling to shed unwanted kilos seek quick and effortless solutions, often bouncing from one weight loss diet to another. Sadly, quick-fix diets just don't produce lasting benefits and are often not very nutritionally balanced.

Avoid crash diets. Although you might see quick results at first, study after study has shown that the benefits are not long term. You'll have better long-term results if you drop 'diets' altogether and take up a healthy eating program today that will serve you throughout your entire life.

Alcohol as part of a healthy lifestyle

Studies have shown that there are natural health-promoting chemicals in wine that may have a protective effect against heart disease and cancer. These natural disease-fighting substances have been shown to have powerful antioxidant properties that are most concentrated in the skins of grapes (red wine has the highest concentration of these).

If taking an occasional glass of wine as part of a delicious meal pleases you and adds richness to your life, enjoy! However, it is important to remember that excess alcohol can have damaging effects on almost every system and cell in the body and can contribute to serious illnesses affecting the nervous system, so follow Nature's lead—everything in moderation.

How to have a happier, healthier mind and body

We've been concentrating on what to eat, how and when, but a healthy lifestyle requires a 'whole body' approach which also includes a sensible approach to exercise and strengthening that mind/body connection through meditation.

Exercise

Regular exercise will help you to burn fat and feel better within yourself. You will benefit more from regular, light exercise than occasional bursts of intense exercise. Walking around the block once each day with longer walks added now and then can have a positive effect on your metabolism. Studies show that short bursts of activity burn carbohydrates, while longer, ongoing exercise burns fat. Like eating, exercising your body should be enjoyable. If you over-exercise or force yourself to do exercise you don't enjoy you risk injuries and can create emotional stress—which is exactly what you are trying to avoid!

Exercise between 6–10am and 6–10pm when your body is stronger and more tolerant.

Meditation for a balanced life

The best way to deepen that mind/body connection we talked about is to take some time each day to slow down with breathing and meditation. When people think of meditation they sometimes think of a long-haired guru sitting under a tree chanting, but **meditation is a powerful tool** that is being incorporated more and more as a valuable part of mainstream life.

There are many wonderful classes including Pilates and Yoga classes that will help you with meditation. There are also countless guided meditations available on CD and DVD that can help you with the process, or you may like to just take 20 minutes each day (preferably at the same time) to do the following:

Simple Meditation Exercise

1. Sit in a quiet space with your back straight. If this is physically impossible, you can lay on the floor with your legs bent at the knees to keep your spine straight on the floor.

2. Pay attention to your breath as it flows in and out, in and out.

3. To relax more, take deeper breaths.

4. On the in-breath think the word 'peace'; on the out-breath think the word 'peace'.

5. Thoughts will come into your mind; don't try to push them away, just let them go and return to focusing on breathing in and out.

6. Do this for 20 minutes and you will notice a deeper sense of calm.

7. You might also like to spend some of this time imagining yourself happier, healthier, preparing nutritious meals and bursting with energy.

8. You can set a quiet alarm to tell you when 20 minutes is over. After you have been meditating for a while you will find that you will gradually open your eyes when it is time to go on with your day.

By incorporating these simple food preparation techniques, changing your attitude to food and including exercise and light meditation in your day, you will see positive results and enjoy the benefits of this simple approach to happier and healthier living.

May you live a long, healthy, happy and abundant life.

Contents

Breakfast

According to Ayurveda (Ah-your-vey-duuh): **'We are what we eat!'**
*This ancient branch of science believes most of the common
ailments are a result of* **poor nutrition** *...*
Any anomaly in the body is thought to emanate in the digestive system.

What's interesting is that this belief is over 5,000 years old!

Apricot Oats

SERVES 1

A recipe from John Kerr.

- ½ cup instant porridge
- 1½ cups milk
- 4 dried apricots, chopped
- 2 tsp. golden syrup

Simmer the porridge and milk together in a small saucepan for 4–5
minutes until slightly thickened and smooth, stirring frequently. Stir
the golden syrup into the porridge. Pour the mixture into a bowl then
sprinkle apricots on top and serve.

Berry Porridge

SERVES 1

- ½ cup (65g) fresh blueberries
- ½ cup (65g) fresh raspberries
- 2 tbs. organic raw sugar
- ⅓ cup semolina

Reserve a few of the berries for garnish, and puree the remainder with 2 cups of water. Strain the mixture through a sieve into a small saucepan. Add sugar and a pinch of salt to the pan and place over medium heat. Bring the puree to the boil, then gently whisk in the semolina, taking care the mixture does not boil over. Reduce the heat as far as possible, and leave the mixture to simmer for about 20 minutes, stirring frequently, until thickened. Serve garnished with reserved berries.

Bircher Muesli

SERVES 2

- ½ apple, peeled, cored and finely grated
- ½ cup apple muesli
- 1 cup pear juice
- 2 kiwi fruit, diced

Place apple, muesli and juice in a bowl. Mix well and leave to soak for 1 hour or overnight in fridge. Top with kiwi fruit.

Optional: Stir through a dollop of your favourite yoghurt.

Cherry & Raspberry Smoothie

SERVES 4

Recipe by Jules Boag.

- *400g cherries, destoned and partially frozen*
- *1 banana, sliced and partially frozen*
- *2 cups freshly squeezed orange juice*
- *⅔ cup raspberry yoghurt*

Place all cherries and banana in a blender and pulse a few times. Add juice and yoghurt and 8 cubes of ice. Blend well, pour into glasses for a *nutritious, delicious* start to the day!

Cinnamon Pancakes

MAKES 8

- *1 cup (175g) organic self raising flour*
- *1 cup (250ml) milk*
- *1 free range egg, beaten*
- *1 tbs. cinnamon*

Lightly whisk all ingredients together. Heat a small non-stick frying pan, pour in enough batter to coat most of the base and over a medium heat cook until bubbles form. Flip and cook until golden on the underside.

Optional: Serve drizzled with honey.

Tip: When added to food, cinnamon inhibits bacterial growth and food spoilage, making it a natural food preservative.

Date & Walnut Porridge

SERVES 1

- ½ cup oats
- 2 dates, chopped
- 1½ cups (375ml) milk
- 3 walnuts, coarsely crushed

Cook oats and dates in milk in a saucepan over medium heat. Stir constantly for 4–5 minutes or until slightly thickened. Sprinkle with walnuts to serve.

Egg White Omelette with Mushrooms

SERVES 2

- 250g mushrooms, washed and sliced
- 1 tsp. sunflower oil
- 4 free range egg whites

Heat a non-stick frying pan. Add ½ tsp. oil then sauté mushrooms until soft, season and set aside. Meanwhile, whisk the egg whites until frothy, but not forming peaks, add remaining oil and heat before pouring in the omelette mixture. Cook over low-medium heat for 2–3 minutes, or until the bottom is firm. Flip the omelette and cook for another 2–3 minutes until the bottom has just set. Top with the sautéed mushrooms.

Fetta Eggs on Toast

SERVES 2

Recipe from Eli Nacson Snr & Leon. Great to see a father teaching his son how to cook.

- *2 tbs. olive oil*
- *40g fetta cheese*
- *3 hard boiled free range eggs*
- *2 slices of thick, wholemeal bread*

Place the oil in a soup bowl and mash in the fetta (add more if you prefer your food salty). Then mash in the eggs and mix together well. Season with pepper or chilli powder (optional) to taste. Toast the slices of bread and spread the mixture across each slice.

Tip: Leon says "My dad was a motor mechanic and this was our favourite breakfast to get him off to work on a full stomach and me off to school many moons ago."

Ginger Yoghurt with Tropical Fruit

SERVES 2

- *200g Greek yoghurt*
- *2 large ripe bananas, frozen*
- *2 tsp. freshly grated ginger*
- *1 papaya, peeled, sliced and chilled*

Blend together yoghurt, bananas and ginger. Spoon into a serving bowl over papaya.

Grape Apple Pear Juice

SERVES 4

- 2 apples
- 2 pears
- 12 grapes
- ⅛ tsp. cinnamon

Wash the fruit and remove the cores. Cut into small pieces and pass through the juicer. Add a sprinkling of cinnamon and serve with crushed ice.

Hint: A good way to break the habit of skipping breakfast is to make and drink fresh fruit or vegetable juices. Rehydrating the body with fresh, natural and nourishing fluids will help you get a head start on a busy day.

Grapefruit with Honey

SERVES 4

- 1 tsp. honey
- ¼ tsp. ground ginger
- ½ tsp. ground cardamom
- 1 grapefruit, peeled and sliced flat circles

Mix first three ingredients and drizzle over slices of grapefruit.

Hawaiian Breakfast

SERVES 4

A recipe from the inspiring Wayne Dyer.

- *2 oranges*
- *2 tbs. honey*
- *1 mango*
- *½ pineapple*

Since I now spend so much of my time in Hawaii, I have taken to eating whatever is fresh and in season. This is my favourite breakfast and it's so simple. Cut oranges in half and juice, then strain. In a tbs. hot water, dissolve the honey then combine orange juice. Slice and cube the mango and pineapple and mix all the ingredients in a bowl.

Herbal Fruit Salad Dressing

- *1 twig mint, finely chopped*
- *1 tsp. freshly grated ginger*
- *1 tsp. fresh lemon juice*
- *1 tsp. honey*

Simply mix together and toss through a freshly cut fruit salad ...
A delicious way to start the day!

Herb Omelette

SERVES 1

- *2 free range eggs*
- *1 tsp. chopped fresh parsley*
- *1 tsp. chopped fresh basil*
- *1 tsp. garlic infused olive oil*

Break the eggs into a bowl, season with sea salt and pepper and whisk well. Add herbs and mix. Heat the oil in a small, non-stick frying pan. Pour in the egg mixture. When the eggs look almost cooked, use a heat proof spatula to fold the omelette in half. Serve immediately.

Lemon & Ginger Infused Honey

MAKES 1 CUP

- *1 cup honey*
- *Zest of 1 lemon*
- *1 tsp. freshly grated ginger*

Place honey in a double boiler with hot water in bottom. Add lemon zest and ginger. Bring water to a boil for 8–10 minutes. Remove from heat and let stand for a further 10 minutes. Strain while still warm. Place in sterilized jars and seal tightly.

Optional: This is just delish in hot and cold teas, served on toast of a morning, drizzled over pancakes, or to coat a roasting chicken or fish at the end of cooking. Substitute lemon for lime or orange for variation.

Mango & Lychee Fruit Salad

SERVES 2–4

- *2 mangoes*
- *24 lychees, peeled*
- *½ lime*
- *6 fresh mint leaves*

Slice the cheeks off the mango and dice the flesh. Pop into a serving bowl and add lychees. Drizzle with the juice of half a lime and gently toss. Cover and chill in the fridge for at least 20 minutes, to allow the flavours time to mingle. Just before serving, shred mint and stir into the salad. Garnish with a few mint sprigs and serve.

Tip: Fruit will provide you with a boost of slow-release energy to keep you going all morning.

Poached Egg & Vegetable Stack

SERVES 4

- *2 roma tomatoes, cut length ways*
- *4 field mushrooms, washed and stems removed*
- *4 free range eggs*
- *4 slices gruyere cheese*

Preheat oven 180°C. On a baking tray lay tomatoes and mushrooms and cook for 15 minutes. Remove and place each mushroom in the middle of a serving plate. Lay tomato on top and keep warm in the oven. Poach eggs, place each on top of tomato before topping with cheese. Grill lightly until melted, season and serve warm.

Tip: When poaching eggs use a deep saucepan. Fill it half with water and bring to a rapid boil. Crack an egg into the water and with a spoon whirlpool the water around the egg to create an even oval shape. Allow to cook for 2–3 minutes with the whites becoming firm and the yolk soft to the touch.

Scrambled Eggs with Raisins

SERVES 2–3

A delicious recipe inspired by Edward de Bono.

- *1 tsp. ghee*
- *½ cup (85g) organic raisins*
- *¼ (62ml) cup milk*
- *4 free range eggs*

Heat ghee in a non-stick frying pan, when melted add raisins and sauté for 2–3 minutes, stirring frequently. While raisins are cooking, whisk milk and eggs in a bowl. Pour the mixture over the raisins and scramble. Serve hot with toast for a yummy breakfast or snack.

Optional: Add a dash of cinnamon.

Scrambled Tofu

SERVES 2

- *1 small tomato, chopped*
- *1 tbs. turmeric*
- *200g tofu, broken into pieces*
- *4 chives, chopped*

Heat a non-stick frying pan over medium heat. Add tomato and turmeric and sauté for 1 minute. Add tofu and stir, cook until evenly coloured and still slightly moist (about 1–1½ minutes, do not let tofu dry out or overcook). Season with sea salt and pepper. Turn tofu onto plates and serve sprinkled with chives.

Summer Berry Breakfast

SERVES 1

Recipe by Michelle Tuite.

- *2 slices spicy fruit loaf*
- *4 tbs. ricotta cheese*
- *2 tbs. blueberries*
- *4 sliced strawberries*

Make a sweet summer breakfast by spreading ricotta chesse over slices of spicy fruit loaf. Top with fresh blueberries and strawberries.

Tip: Remember to always wash your fruit and vegetables before cooking or eating.

Stewed Apples & Pears

SERVES 2

- *1 apple*
- *1 pear*
- *1 tbs. organic raisins*
- *1 clove*

Peel and chop apple and pear into small pieces. Place in a small saucepan and add ¼ cup water. Add raisins and clove. Bring to boil and reduce to a simmer. Cook for about 20 minutes or until the fruit is of a tender consistency.

Optional: This is a sensational breakfast served warm with a dollop of natural yoghurt and drizzled with honey.

Stewed Prunes with Yoghurt

SERVES 4

- *250g pitted prunes*
- *½ cup (125ml) orange juice*
- *½ tsp. cinnamon*
- *½ cup Greek yoghurt*

Soak prunes in 1 cup of water over night in the refrigerator. Remove, pour into a saucepan, add orange juice and cinnamon. Over high heat bring to the boil, reduce heat and let simmer for 20–25 minutes. Cool before serving with a dollop of fresh Greek Yoghurt.

Tip: Prunes contain a lot of fibres and 'sorbitol' a stool loosening sugar. They also help to slow the ageing process of the brain and body and are extremely good for increasing one's vitality.

Tropical Breakfast Risotto

SERVES 4

- *1 cup (185g) arborio rice*
- *400ml can coconut milk*
- *¼ cup (45g) organic raisins*
- *1 cup chopped, firm banana*

In a medium saucepan, bring 2 cups of water and rice to the boil. Reduce heat to medium-low and simmer uncovered, stirring frequently for creaminess. When the water has been absorbed, add the can of coconut milk. As that gets absorbed, but while still creamy, fold through raisins and banana. Heat for another 2–3 minutes and serve when rice is tender.

Optional: This is lovely with a variety of tropical fruits; papaya, mango, passionfruit and pineapple and sprinkled with some toasted, flaked almonds for a crunchy finish.

Tip: This dish should be creamy and moist, if too thick, stir in a little more water before adding raisins and bananas.

Walnut Butter

MAKES 1 CUP

- *1½ cups toasted walnuts*
- *1 tbs. (15ml) olive oil or as needed*
- *1 tsp. raw honey or maple syrup*

Preheat oven 200°C. Spread walnuts on a baking sheet and bake for 5 minutes or until fragrant and lightly browned. In a small food processor, place the walnuts and start the machine. In a slow and steady drizzle, pour in the olive oil. If after 1 tbs. it isn't coming together, pour in 1 tsp. at a time until it does. Stop the machine often to scrape down the sides. When it forms a "*butter*" add honey and a pinch of salt then stop the machine.

Hint: Walnut is an excellent nut containing protein, iron and essential fatty acids. Use this spread on toast, pancakes, or in cookie recipes!

Tip: Toasting nuts enhances their flavour and crunch.

Morning & Afternoon Teas

You are as happy as you make up your mind to be.

Anonymous

A Healthy Snack

SERVES 2

Recipe from Jimmy Barnes.

- *1 pawpaw (papaya), peeled and deseeded*
- *1 banana*
- *½ a lime, juiced*
- *½ an orange, juiced*

Whenever I feel like a quick snack, Jane usually cuts up a pawpaw in slices and chops up a banana, throws them into a bowl then pours a little orange and lime juice on top. Deepak once told me that pawpaw is known in some parts of the world as the 'medicine tree' because it's full of a powerful enzyme called Papain and Vitamin A and C. That's interesting ... *But Jane and I eat it because it tastes good!*

Almond Stuffed Dates

MAKES 24

- *24 blanched almonds*
- *24 (about 400g) fresh dates*

Preheat oven to 180°C. Scatter the almonds over a baking tray and bake for 6 minutes or until toasted. Whilst cooling, use a small, sharp knife to cut a slit in each date. Remove stones. Insert an almond in each cavity. Arrange on a serving platter to serve.

Hint: Bursting with natural goodness, sun-ripened dates are among the most delectable sources of fibre, potassium and other essential nutrients. It is rumoured that 'One never forgets one's first date!"

Banana Bread

MAKES 1 LOAF
Four words ... BAKE IT! It's fantastic!

- *2 large ripe bananas, mashed*
- *¾ cup sugar*
- *1 cup (260g) whole egg mayonnaise*
- *2 cups (350g) self raising flour*

Preheat oven 180°C. Line a loaf tin with baking paper. In a medium bowl, add bananas and sugar and stir. Add mayonnaise, sifted flour and a pinch of salt then lightly mix, until just combined. Pour into tin and cook for 50—60 minutes or until a skewer, inserted into the middle, comes out clean. Allow to cool for 10 minutes, then turn onto wire rack.

Optional: Add 2 tbs. of golden syrup when mixing bananas and sugar. To liven after a couple of days, toast and serve dolloped with mascarpone and drizzled with Berry Blast (see: Sauces, Salsas & Marinades) for breakfast ... YUM SCRUM!

Blueberry & Ginger Muffins

MAKES 12

Recipe from Vanessa Sheldrick ... D.i.v.i.n.e!

- 2 cups (350g) self raising flour
- 2 tsp. ground ginger
- 2 cups (500ml) cream
- ½ cup fresh blueberries

Preheat oven 200°C. Sift flour into a bowl, add ginger and mix into a well. Pour in cream and add blueberries. Mix gently until mixture has combined. Spoon batter into patty-paper lined muffin tins ⅔ full. Bake for 15–20 minutes or until lightly golden on top.

Tip: The best utensil for mixing muffins is a wooden spoon. Be careful not to overmix as it reduces its ability to rise.

Camembert Sandwich

MAKES 2

A recipe from Barry Crocker who recommends this "As a delicious snack in the middle of the afternoon to keep you going until dinner."

- 4 crunchy crackers
- 2 slices of camembert cheese
- 1 lettuce leaf, halved
- 4 thin slices of cucumber

Simply spread the cheese onto two crackers, lay lettuce on top add two cucumber slices to each then place the other cracker on top.

Citrus Raisin Loaf

SERVES 12

This came from an author talk at the fabulous Mt. Barker Library, South Australia.

- 1 cup (170g) organic raisins
- ½ tsp. mixed spice
- 1 cup (250ml) orange juice
- 1 cup (175g) self raising flour

Preheat oven 180°C. Soak raisins and mixed spice in juice overnight. Stir in self raising flour. Line a loaf tin with baking paper and scrape mixture into it. Bake for 40–45 minutes.

Tip: Raisins are a natural burst of sweetness in baked goods, confectionary, snacks, cereals, sauces, condiments, curries and casseroles too.

Coconut Pikelets

MAKES 14

These are very tasty!

- 475ml coconut milk
- 2 cups (350g) self raising flour
- 2 tbs. organic raw sugar
- 2 free range eggs

Combine all ingredients with ½ cup water, and gently whisk until smooth. Pour a small amount of mixture into a hot, non-stick frypan and cook over medium heat until bubbles appear. Flip and cook until lightly browned.

Date Loaf

SERVES 12

- ¾ cup dates, chopped
- 6 tbs. (90g) softened butter
- 2 free range eggs
- 1 cup (200g) wholemeal self raising flour

Combine dates and ⅓ cup of boiled water in a bowl and allow to stand for 30 minutes. Beat butter until light, add eggs one at a time beating until just combined (between additions mixture will separate but will come together later). Add butter to dates mix, stir in flour in two batches. Scrape into a baking paper lined loaf tin and bake for 40–45 minutes at 180°C.

Optional: Serve with maple butter made from whipping butter until light and adding to it maple syrup.

Fruit Tarts

MAKES 6

- 6 slices raisin bread, crusts removed and slightly flattened
- 2 x 125g tubs of vanilla crème fraiche
- 1 cup diced kiwi fruit
- 1 cup sliced strawberries

Press bread slices into muffin pans and blind bake for 6 minutes or until golden. Allow to cool. Dollop equal quantities of crème fraiche into each case and top with mixed fruit.

Golf Bag Trail Mix

SERVES 1

A recipe from the vibrant Kerri-Anne Kennerly.

- ¼ cup macadamia
- ¼ cup sultanas
- ¼ cup dried apricots
- ¼ cup pecan halves

Kerri-Anne said "Whenever I am out on the golf course and I really need something to keep me going, this snack works wonders! In a bowl mix everything together and pop into a small zip lock bag. Whatever is left over, I place in an air tight container ready for my next under par adventure!"

Herbamare Seasoned Crackers

SERVES 1

A recipe from the beautiful Miranda Kerr.

- *2 brown rice/seaweed/tamari rice crackers*
- *½ an avocado*
- *Herbamare seasoning*

Place two crackers on a plate and spread avocado on each cracker. Sprinkle with the seasoning. This is an incredibly delicious and nutritious snack.

Tip: Herbamare is a natural seasoning made of sea salt, celery stalk, celery leaves, leeks, watercress, garden cress, onions, chives, parsley, lovage, garlic, basil, marjoram, rosemary, thyme, kelp ... It can be used to flavour soups, savouries and mains and can be bought from most health food stores.

Jaffa Lychees

MAKES 16

Easy *and* elegant.

- *100g dark chocolate*
- *1 tbs. orange rind, finely zested*
- *16 fresh lychees, peeled and deseeded*

Melt chocolate, add zest and stir. Coat lychees well, place on a baking paper lined tray and refrigerate until ready to serve.

Tip: Substitute orange zest for finely chopped chilli, it is a lovely contrast to the coolness of the lychee.

Macadamia Nut Pie Crust

MAKES 1

- *180g macadamia nuts*
- *2 free range eggs, whisked*
- *1½ cups soy flour*

Preheat the oven to 180°C. Process macadamia nuts until they reach a peanut butter like consistency. Scrape out into a bowl, stir in eggs and flour until well blended. Line a 20cm cake tin base with baking paper. Press the mixture into the bottom and up the sides. Bake for 5 minutes or until light golden brown.

Tip: Use in any sweet recipe calling for a prebaked pie base or crust.

Mango Friands

MAKES 12

- 4 egg whites
- 1 cup (150g) icing sugar mixture
- 2 cups (340g) almond meal
- 200g tub mango yoghurt

Preheat oven to 180°C. Use an electric beater to whisk egg whites in a large, clean, dry bowl until peaks form. Gently stir through icing sugar and almond meal until just combined. Fold through yoghurt and spoon mixture evenly into paper lined friand holes. Bake for 25 minutes or until cooked. Set aside for 2 minutes. Turn out onto a wire rack to cool.

Optional: Change the flavour by changing the yoghurt.

Mango Fruit Cake

SEVERS 8-10

Recipe from Yvonne Hackenberg.

- 1kg mixed fruit
- 2 cups fresh mango pulp and juice
- 2 cups (350g) self raising flour
- 1½ cups macadamia nuts, roughly chopped

Soak mixed fruit in mango pulp and juice and ¼ cup of water overnight. Preheat oven 125°C. Stir in self raising flour and nuts, pour mixture into a 22cm cake tin lined with baking paper and bake for 2–2 ½ hours.

Tip: This can be frozen.

4 Ingredients Fast, Fresh & Healthy

Dips, Dressings & Sauces

A truly rich man is one whose children run into his arms when his hands are empty

Author Unknown

Dips

Avocado & Cumin Dip

SERVES 4

- *2 avocados, mashed*
- *1 lime, juiced*
- *1–2 tsp. ground, roasted cumin seeds*

Mix all ingredients together. Serve with favourite croutons, savoury biscuits or a mezze of fresh vegie sticks.

Beetroot Ricotta Chickpea

SERVES 4–6

- *1 beetroot, trimmed*
- *200g chickpeas*
- *2 lemons, juiced*
- *100g ricotta*

In a medium pot, boil beetroot in water for 30–40 minutes, add chickpeas and cook for a further 10 minutes, until soft. Drain, place in a food processor and blend, add lemon juice. Place in a medium bowl, add ricotta and mix through. Season and serve.

Char-Grilled Capsicum & Goats Cheese Dip

SERVES 4

- 2 red capsicums, seeded and cut into quarters
- 100g goats cheese
- 1 tbs. (15ml) olive oil
- 1 tbs. chopped parsley

Grill capsicums skin side up until the skin begins to blister. Cover and allow to cool before peeling the capsicum skin from its flesh. Place the flesh in a food processor or blender along with the goats cheese and olive oil, season with sea salt and pepper. Blend until fully combined. Scrape into a serving bowl. Chill and sprinkle with fresh parsley when ready to serve.

Cheesy Almond Dip

SERVES 4

- 125g white castello cheese
- 250g cream cheese
- 8 drops tabasco sauce
- 125g flaked almonds, toasted

Blend castello and cream cheese in a food processor, add tabasco and blend well. Spoon mixture into a flat serving bowl and sprinkle generously with flaked almonds. Chill in fridge for about 20 minutes before serving.

Optional: Serve garnished with a fresh green basil leaf and lots of fresh carrot sticks.

Creamy Beetroot Dip

MAKES 2 CUPS

A recipe from Carly Nelson.

- 1 beetroot, trimmed
- 1 tbs. Dijon Mustard or horseradish cream
- ½ cup cream cheese
- ½ cup dukkah spice blend

Bring beetroot to the boil in a saucepan. Reduce heat and cook for 30–40 minutes or until soft. Drain and allow to cool. Blend beetroot and mustard, add cream cheese and dukkah. Spoon into serving bowl then let chill so cream cheese can set or thicken and serve with Lebanese crisps.

Tip: Beetroot's main benefits are that it contains no fat, very few calories and is a great source of fibre. Beetroot has for many years been used as a treatment for cancer in Europe. Specific anti-carcinogens are bound to the red colouring matter which supposedly helps fight against cancer. Beetroot also increases the uptake of oxygen by as much as 400 per cent.

Duck Liver Pate

MAKES 2 CUPS

- *450g duck livers*
- *200g butter, melted*
- *3 tbs. (50ml) double cream*
- *1 tbs. brandy*

Heat a heavy-based frying pan over a medium heat. Pour a little of the melted butter into the hot pan, add half the duck livers and cook for three minutes. The livers should be cooked on the outside and pink in the middle. Transfer them to a plate and repeat with the rest of the livers. Pour the brandy into the fry pan and gently bring to the boil. Transfer the livers to a food processor and blend them for a minute or so until smooth. Pour in the brandy, the remaining butter and cream and blend once more. Season with sea salt and freshly ground black pepper. Serve chilled.

Fetta Dip

MAKES 2 CUPS

- *500g Danish fetta*
- *3 lemons, juiced*
- *100ml Greek yoghurt*
- *8 tbs. fresh chopped parsley*

Place all ingredients in a food processor and blend. Season with cracked black pepper.

Guacamole

SERVES 4

- *2 avocados, mashed with a fork*
- *1 clove garlic, crushed*
- *1 tbs. freshly chopped coriander*
- *1 tsp. freshly chopped chilli*

Lightly mash avocados, add remaining ingredients. Mix and serve with corn chips, crackers, carrot or celery sticks.

Tip: Avocados are a treasure trove of vital nutrients needed for a healthy body. They contain vitamin C, which is an amazing antioxidant, anti-viral and anti-bacterial. Vitamin K which is an antioxidant that helps protect the liver from free radicals damage and amino acids that help increase the body's production of glutathione which is said to inhibit the progression of the aging process.

Indian Dip

MAKES 1 CUP

Recipe by Louise Budd ... Fast and fabulous!

- *½ cup plain yoghurt*
- *½ tsp. cumin*
- *½ tsp. ground coriander*
- *3 tbs. finely chopped fresh cucumber*

Mix together yoghurt and spices. Stir in cucumber and serve with pappadums or as a topper on Indian mains.

Olive Tapenade

MAKES 1¾ CUPS

- 3 cups kalamata olives, drained
- 8 anchovies
- 3 tbs. freshly chopped parsley
- 3 tbs. (45ml) garlic infused olive oil

Place all ingredients in a food processor and puree. Season with pepper. Chill prior to serving.

Pea & Mint Dip

MAKES 1 CUP

Recipe by Michelle Ashdown.

- ½ cup peas
- 4–5 small mint leaves
- 1 tbs. cream cheese
- ½–1 tsp. fresh lemon juice

Steam peas until tender. Using a handheld mixer, blend with 1 tsp. boiling water. Add mint, stir in cream cheese and lemon juice.

Roasted Eggplant & Goats Cheese Dip

SERVES 4

- ½ cup (125ml) garlic infused olive oil
- 1 fresh eggplant, cut in half
- 200g goats cheese
- ½ cup pine nuts, toasted

Preheat oven 200°C. Pour ½ the oil into a bowl and toss in eggplant. Season with salt and pepper. Wrap eggplant with foil till completely covered. Place in oven for 40 minutes. Remove, unwrap foil and scrape out the eggplant into a food processor so that just the skin remains. Add rest of ingredients and process. Season to taste.

Smoked Salmon Pate

SERVES 4

- 200g canned cannellini beans, drained
- 2 tbs. chopped dill
- 1 lemon, juiced
- 200g smoked salmon

Blend all ingredients in a food processor until smooth. Add sea salt and pepper to taste. Transfer to a bowl and chill for at least 30 minutes prior to serving.

Optional: Serve with Melba Toast (see: 4 Ingredients), crackers or fresh vegie sticks.

Salad Dressings

No matter how far you've gone down the wrong path, TURN BACK!

Anonymous

Basil Lemon Dressing

MAKES ½ CUP

- *2 tbs. Dijon mustard*
- *1 lemon, juiced*
- *6 tbs. extra virgin olive oil*
- *16 basil leaves, very thinly sliced*

Combine all ingredients in a small jar. Season well with sea salt and pepper. Cover and shake well before drizzling over your favourite salad.

Caramelised Balsamic Dressing

MAKES ½ CUP

Recipe by Angie Covino.

- *2 cups (500ml) balsamic vinegar*
- *½ cup organic raw sugar*
- *1 cinnamon stick*
- *2 cloves*

Place all ingredients in a saucepan and bring to the boil. Reduce heat and simmer for 10–15 minutes or until it reduces slightly. Remove from heat, strain and allow to completely cool (it will continue to thicken as it cools). Pour into a jar and store in the refrigerator until required.

Herb Dressing

MAKES ½ CUP

- *4 tbs. freshly chopped parsley*
- *4 tbs. (60ml) apple juice*
- *1 tsp. mild mustard*
- *1 tbs. (15ml) cider vinegar*

Place all the ingredients into a food processor and blend until smooth. Season to taste.

Honey Lemon Dressing

MAKES ¾ CUP

- *½ cup (125ml) extra virgin olive oil*
- *2 tbs. honey*
- *1 lemon, juice and zest*

Mix altogether, whisk and season.

Optional: Delicious drizzled over the Rosemary Chicken Skewers (see: Light Lunches).

Italian Vinaigrette

MAKES 1½ CUPS

- 1 cup (250ml) extra virgin olive oil
- 2 tbs. mixed dry herbs
- ⅓ cup (85ml) white balsamic vinegar
- 1 tbs. Dijon mustard

In a medium pan place half the oil, bring to a medium heat and add the dried herbs. After 3 minutes take from heat and cool, this allows time for the flavours to infuse. Add remaining ingredients, and mix. Can be stored in bottles or jars.

Lemon Thyme Dressing

MAKES 1½ CUPS

- ⅓ cup (85ml) lemon juice
- 1 tbs. fresh thyme leaves
- 2 tsp. Dijon mustard
- 1 cup (250ml) extra virgin olive oil

Mix altogether and shake well. Store in a refrigerator.

Lychee & Mint Dressing

MAKES 1 CUPS

This is *soooo* very yummy!

- *12 fresh lychees, peeled and seeded*
- *6–8 mint leaves, chopped*
- *¼ cup (62ml) rice wine vinegar*
- *¼ – ½ cup peanut oil*

Combine the lychees, mint and vinegar in a blender and purée on low speed. Slowly add the oil until emulsified. Season to taste. Add just enough dressing to coat your favourite salad. Store remaining dressing in a tightly sealed jar in the refrigerator.

Hint: To sterilise a jar prior to use, place it in a large pot of boiling water for a couple of minutes.

Parsley & Lemon Salad Dressing

MAKES ½ CUP

- *2 tbs. (30ml) olive oil*
- *2 tbs. (30ml) lemon juice*
- *2 tsp. brown sugar*
- *1 tsp. freshly cut parsley*

Place oil and juice with brown sugar and parsley into a screw top jar. Shake jar well. Pour over salad to serve and enjoy!

Tip: Long before the invention of after dinner mints people ate parsley to remove bad breath. Traces of this tradition can still be seen today as parsley is often used as garnish (next time don't leave it … Eat it!)

Pineapple Chilli Dressing

MAKES APPROX. 2 CUPS

- 2 cups freshly chopped pineapple
- 1 chilli, sliced, seeds removed and then chopped
- 4 tbs. coriander
- 1 lemon, juiced

Place all ingredients in a blender and puree. Season with salt and pepper.

Hint: This is SENSATIONAL served over grilled fish or chicken. There are many health benefits of pineapple. Its nutrients include calcium, potassium, fibre, and vitamin C. Not to mention that it is both low in fat and cholesterol.

Tip: Errol McCosker says "A pineapple is ripe when you tug on a leaf and it pulls from the fruit easily."

Fresh Thai Dressing

MAKES ¼ CUP

Y.u.m.m.y!

- 1 tbs. Gourmet Garden Thai blend
- 1 tbs. (15ml) fish sauce
- 1 tbs. brown sugar or palm sugar
- 1 lime, juiced

Pop all ingredients into a jar, seal and shake well to combine.

Optional: This is SCRUMPTIOUS tossed through a fresh Asian salad with glass noodles and topped with either thinly sliced beef, grilled chicken or cooked prawns.

Tomato Herb Dressing

SERVES 4–6

- *2 cups semi dried tomatoes, chopped with their oil*
- *300ml red wine vinegar*
- *1 tbs. Dijon mustard*
- *6 tbs. freshly chopped parsley*

Place all ingredients in a bowl and mix. Season with cracked black pepper and sea salt. A great topping for fish and chicken recipes.

Verjuice Dressing

Inspired by the beautiful Dominique Rizzo, Primary Industry Week 2010.

- *1 clove garlic, crushed*
- *1 tbs. (15ml) white wine vinegar*
- *3 tbs. (45ml) olive oil*
- *2 tbs. (30ml) verjuice*

Whisk together all the ingredients and season with sea salt and pepper.

Optional: Verjuice (or 'vertjus' in French meaning "green juice") is very acidic and is made by pressing unripe grapes. It can be expensive, but a little goes a long way and its uses are many and varied. We use it to deglaze pans after cooking fish or chicken to create a tangy sauce from the reduced juices. It can also be used to marinate, to dress oysters or salads instead of lemon or vinegar, or even as a zesty cordial mixed with soda or tonic.

Sauces, Salsas & Marinades

Friendship has great resources for it consists of two hearts.

Anonymous

Avocado Salsa

SERVES 4

A spectacular little recipe by Jeff Thode.

- *2 ripe avocados*
- *½ red onion, finely diced*
- *¼ bunch coriander, chopped*
- *2 tbs. freshly squeezed lemon juice*

Peel and dice avocado into 1 cm cubes. Add onion and coriander. Drizzle with lemon juice to taste and season as desired.

Optional: Serve with a plate of freshly cut carrot sticks.

Tip: If preparing ahead of time, return seed to dip to stop discolouration. Cover and place in refrigerator until ready to serve.

Basil Pesto

MAKES 1 CUP

- *2 cups fresh basil leaves, packed*
- *⅓ cup pine nuts*
- *½ cup (125ml) extra virgin olive oil*
- *½ cup (70g) freshly grated parmesan cheese*

Combine basil and pine nuts in a blender and pulse a few times. Slowly add the oil in a constant stream while the blender is on. Stop to scrape down the sides with a spatula. Add the cheese and pulse again until blended. Season with a pinch of sea salt and freshly ground pepper to taste.

Optional: Add 2 garlic cloves with pine nuts.

Hint: Serve with pasta, baked potatoes, or spread over toasted baguette slices topped with fresh slices of tomato.

Berry Blast

MAKES 2 CUPS

Recipe by Spud Moore.

- *1 cup blueberries*
- *1 cup raspberries*
- *1 cup strawberries*
- *1 tbs. organic raw sugar*

Place all berries into a non stick saucepan with enough water to almost cover the berries. Bring to the boil and stir until the berries have softened (around 4 minutes). Reduce heat and stir in sugar. Allow to simmer for a further 2 minutes. This is the best sauce accompanying pancakes, banana bread or as a gorgeous topping over ice cream.

Tip: You can keep this sauce in a covered jug or sealed container in the fridge for up to two weeks.

Chilli & Honey Dressing

MAKES ½ CUP

- 1 birdseye chilli, seeds removed and chopped
- 2 tbs. honey
- 2 limes, juiced (approx. ¼ cup)
- 2 tsp. grated fresh ginger

Combine all ingredients together and mix.

Hint: This is delicious drizzled over grilled chicken, fish and salads.

Coriander Pesto

MAKES APPROX. 1 CUP

- 100g fresh coriander leaves, chopped
- 2 tbs. pine nuts
- ⅓ cup (85ml) olive oil
- ¼ cup (35g) freshly grated parmesan cheese

Pop coriander and pine nuts into a blender and pulse a few times before gradually adding the oil in a steady stream. Add parmesan cheese and blend together until it forms a smooth paste. Use immediately or store in a jar in the refrigerator.

Optional: This is lovely tossed through penne pasta with freshly grilled cherry tomatoes.

Cranberry, Orange & Ginger Sauce

MAKES APPROX. 1 CUP

Sweet, sour and spicy!

- *1 cup dried cranberries*
- *½ an orange, juiced*
- *1cm fresh ginger, peeled and finely chopped*
- *3 tbs. organic raw sugar*

Over a low heat, mix together all ingredients in a saucepan with ¼ cup water. Boil gently until jam-like. As cranberries and ginger soften, mash with a fork.

Tip: Serve this with turkey or roast duck.

Detoxifying Spice Mix

MAKES APPROX. ⅓ CUP

- *1 tsp. turmeric*
- *2 parts cumin powder*
- *3 parts coriander powder*
- *4 parts fennel powder*

Combine together and store in an airtight container.

Hint: These spices are very good for detoxification. The mixture can be used with vegetables, soups or as a rub on fish or chicken or as a base for a delicious marinade.

Dipping Sauce

MAKES ½ CUP

This is such a quick and easy dipping sauce for many dishes.

- *4 tbs. (60ml) sweet chilli sauce*
- *1 lime, zest and juice*
- *1 tbs. finely chopped spring onion*

Mix altogether and serve with grilled prawns or as a fresh, zesty salad dressing with coriander.

Kiwi Salsa

SERVES 4

This is sensational.

- *4 kiwi fruit, peeled and chopped*
- *½ cup pomegranate seeds*
- *½ avocado, diced*
- *½ red onion, finely diced*

Place all ingredients in a medium sized bowl. Season with sea salt and pepper.

Optional: Add some chopped coriander if you have it. This is a fresh, light accompaniment with grilled or poached chicken or fish.

Hint: See Pomegranate & Apple Salad (Salads) for tip on how to remove seeds from the pomegranate easily.

Lemon Wasabi

MAKES ¼ CUP

- *2 tbs. (30ml) fresh lemon juice*
- *1 tsp. wasabi paste*
- *1 tbs. (15ml) fish sauce*
- *1 tsp. sesame oil*

Combine all ingredients together and mix. Add more wasabi if you like a stronger flavour.

Optional: A delicious marinade for prawns, fish or chicken.

Lime Mayonnaise

MAKES 1 CUP

- *1 cup (260g) mayonnaise*
- *1 lime*
- *4 drops tabasco sauce*

Mix together the mayonnaise, 1 tbs. finely grated lime zest, 1½ tbs. lime juice and the tabasco. Season with pepper.

Optional: This is amazing served with almost any seafood, especially prawns, calamari and Crab Cakes (see: Fish & Seafood). Garnish with a wedge of lime.

Mango Mayonnaise

MAKES APPROX. 2 CUPS

Recipe from Jacqui Burnie.

- *1 mango, mashed*
- *1 cup (260g) mayonnaise*

Mix mango and mayonnaise in equal parts.

Hint: Flavoured mayonnaises are a marvelously easy accompaniment to nearly anything. Add colour and flavour with herbs, tomato paste, saffron, turmeric or curry powder. Season with garlic, ginger, spring onions or lemon juice. Mix with Greek yoghurt and season for a sensational salad dressing.

Mint Pesto

MAKES 1 CUP

- *2 bunches of mint*
- *2 tbs. (30ml) extra virgin olive oil*
- *1 cup (160g) roasted almonds, chopped*

Place all in a processor and blend. Scrape down with a spatula and add a little more oil if required.

Optional: Delicious used as a marinade on chicken, as a spread on a sandwich or dolloped on a piece of grilled tuna.

Mango Salsa

MAKES 2 CUPS

- 1 mango, diced
- 1 avocado, diced
- 1 vine-ripened tomato, chopped into 1cm cubes
- ½ red onion, finely chopped

Mix all ingredients together and serve over grilled chicken or fish.

Hint: Mango 'the fruit of India' is a superior source of beta-carotene, in fact it is one of the best sources of beta-carotene (a powerful antioxidant) there is. It is juicy, sweet and versatile. Delicious in fruit salads, green salads or grilled on a BBQ and drizzled with lime for a refreshing dessert.

Mint Salsa

MAKES 2 CUPS

- 2 vine ripened tomatoes, chopped
- 1 small cucumber, diced
- 2 tbs. freshly chopped spring onion
- 1 tsp. mint

Mix tomatoes, cucumber and onion. Season before tossing through mint. Allow to stand for 10 minutes.

Optional: This is scrummy served with chicken kebabs, rice and naan bread ... Enjoy!

Minted Yoghurt

MAKES ¾ CUP

- 1 garlic clove, crushed
- 200g natural yoghurt
- 2 tbs. finely chopped fresh mint

Combine all ingredients together and serve as an accompaniment with curries or as a marinade for chicken, this will not only tenderise but flavour the chicken.

Preserved Lemons

MAKES 1 JAR.

- 5 lemons, very well cleaned
- ½ cup of sea salt
- 4 bay leaves
- 2 cinnamon sticks

Cut lemons lengthways into quarters, keeping bases intact. Rub half the salt into the centre of each lemon. Place bay leaves and cinnamon sticks in the jar then pack the lemons in, squishing them down so that the juice from them rises to the top of the jar. Fill the jar with lemons, make sure the top is covered with lemon juice (add more juice if necessary). Sprinkle with remaining salt. Seal and store in a cool place, away from direct sunlight for six weeks. To use the lemons, remove the flesh and pith and discard. Wash and slice the skin.

Tip: For a 'last minute' version of preserved lemons, simply boil some whole lemons in very salty water for about 30 minutes. The tangy intensity they offer adds loads of flavour to tagines, Moroccan salads, roast chicken, baked fish and loads more.

Quick Tomato Chutney

MAKES 1 CUP

- 3 large ripe tomatoes, chopped
- ½ small brown onion, finely diced
- 2 tbs. brown sugar
- 1 tbs. (15ml) red wine vinegar

In a saucepan, place all ingredients together and cook over a low heat for around 7 minutes.

Optional: Season and serve warm with grilled chicken or fish or cold with a cheese platter or ploughman's lunch.

Red Onion Marmalade

MAKES 1–2 CUPS

- 1 tbs. (15ml) extra virgin olive oil
- 4–5 (250g) red onions, thinly sliced
- ⅔ cup (165ml) chicken stock
- 1½ tbs. balsamic vinegar

Heat the oil in a saucepan, add the onions and cook over medium heat for 2–3 minutes until they start to soften. Add the stock and vinegar, reduce the heat to low, partially cover the pan and simmer for 30–45 minutes stirring frequently, until the onions are very soft and the stock is reduced to a thick syrup. Remove the pan from the heat and allow the marmalade to cool, then cover and refrigerate until needed.

Hint: Great served with a cheese platter and fresh, crusty bread.

Sweet Chilli Mayonnaise

MAKES ¼ CUP

- *⅓ cup (85g) whole egg mayonnaise*
- *1 tbs. (15ml) sweet chilli sauce*
- *1 tbs. chopped chives*

Combine ingredients in a small bowl.

Optional: Delicious served with Golden Baked Chips (see: Potatoes & Rice).

Tahini Sauce

MAKES ½ CUP

- *1 clove garlic, crushed*
- *100ml tahini*
- *1 lemon, juiced*
- *2 tbs. chopped parsley*

Mix garlic with ½ tsp. of sea salt until smooth (may need to pound salt slightly). Add tahini and lemon juice and whisk until sticky, then whisk in 75ml of warm water. When combined stir in the parsley.

Optional: This is lovely trickled over grilled fish.

Tomato Salsa

MAKES 1 CUP

- ⅓ cup (85ml) olive oil
- 1 lemon, juice and a little zest
- 2 tbs. honey
- 2 vine-ripened tomatoes, seeded and finely chopped

Combine first three ingredients in a jug. Season with sea salt and pepper. Stir in tomatoes.

Optional: This is fabulous rubbed into chicken before cooking and used to flavour curries and rice or lentil dishes or as a topper for grilled haloumi.

White Bean Purée

MAKES 1 CUP

- 400g cannellini beans, rinsed and drained
- ¼ cup ground almonds
- 1 tbs. (15ml) lemon juice
- ¼ cup (62ml) garlic infused olive oil

Blend all ingredients in a food processor, season with sea salt and pepper and set aside.

Optional: This is delicious served with Blackened Fish (see: Fish & Seafood).

Cocktail Food

Water is the most neglected nutrient in your diet, but one of the most vital.

Kelly Barton

Baked Camembert

SERVES 4

- *250g wheel of camembert*
- *3–4 garlic cloves, quartered*
- *50g sun-dried tomatoes*
- *2 twigs fresh thyme*

Preheat oven to 150°C. Place camembert on a heat proof serving dish. Score the cheese diagonally, just large enough to wedge garlic segments and semi-dried tomatoes into them. Sprinkle with fresh thyme, season and bake for 10 minutes.

Optional: Serve with thin slices of fresh crusty bread or your favourite crackers.

Tip: Garlic is one of the most beneficial natural food supplements there is. Listed alphabetically the nutrients in garlic are: Calcium, folate, iron, magnesium, manganese, phosphorus, potassium, selenium, vitamin B-1, vitamin B-2, vitamin B-3, vitamin C, and zinc ... Make that 4 cloves of garlic!!!!

Baked Chicken Wings

SERVES 4

This was a recipe given to us by a lovely lady at a book signing in Brisbane, we don't know your name but we *'thank you.'*

- *16 free range chicken wings*
- *2 tbs. all purpose seasoning*
- *1 tbs. lemon pepper*
- *1 tbs. dried oregano*

Preheat oven 180°C. Cover the base of a baking tray with baking paper. Cut the tips off the wings and discard, then cut between the joints. Mix all three dry ingredients together before coating the chicken wings well. Place wings on tray and bake for 30–35 minutes or until golden brown.

Cashews with Caramel Chilli

SERVES 4

- *1 tbs. ghee*
- *¼ cup (80g) honey*
- *1 pinch of chilli powder*
- *2 x 150g pkt raw cashews*

Line a baking tray with baking paper. Melt butter in a frying pan over medium heat. Add the honey and chilli powder with 2 tbs. water and salt to taste, stir whilst bringing to the boil. Add the cashews and cook, stirring for 5 minutes or until golden. Transfer the cashews onto the tray. Set aside to cool completely. Tap the cashew mixture gently to separate before serving.

Crumbed Stuffed Olives

MAKES 24

- 24 fetta stuffed olives
- 1 free range egg, beaten
- ¼ cup breadcrumbs, seasoned with salt and pepper
- 2 cups (500ml) grape seed oil

Dip olives in egg, then in crumb mixture to coat. Lay onto a flat plate and refrigerate for 15 minutes. Repeat process. Heat the oil in a large wok, when hot, deep-fry olives in batches until lightly browned. Drain on absorbent paper.

Optional: Serve olives with a Chilli Aioli, made combining sour cream, sweet chilli sauce and a little garlic.

Cucumber Rounds with Salmon Mousse

MAKES 16

These will be popular.

- 200g smoked salmon
- 125g soft cream cheese
- 1–2 tbs. creme fraiche or sour cream
- 1 cucumber, peeled and sliced into 1cm thick rounds

In a food processor, pulse salmon into a paste. Add cream cheese and crème fraiche and season with pepper. Continue to pulse until smooth. Spoon a teaspoon of the salmon mousse onto each cucumber round. Cover and chill for 10 minutes before serving.

Optional: Serve with a twist of lemon juice or a twig of dill.

Cheese & Herb Log

- ½ tub cream cheese
- 1 tbs. chopped dill
- 1 tbs. chopped fresh chives
- 1 tsp. finely grated lemon rind

Mix all together thoroughly and season to taste. Spoon mixture onto a sheet of baking paper. Shape into a log, roll up firmly and twist ends. Place in the fridge to chill. Serve sliced on crackers or toast triangles.

Date Delights

MAKES 10

- 2 tbs. (50g) soft blue cheese
- 2 tbs. (50g) cream cheese
- 2 tbs. chopped chives
- 10 dates

Mix the first three ingredients together. Remove stones from the dates. Pipe or spoon the mixture into the dates. Chill before serving.

Tip: The sweet and savoury of this dish make it a sensational appetiser served with pre-dinner drinks.

Goats Cheese Croutons

MAKES 12

- *12 slices of fresh French Stick*
- *2–3 tbs. chilli jam*
- *150g herbed goats cheese*
- *12 cherry tomatoes, sliced*

Preheat oven to 180°C. Place bread slices on a paper lined baking tray and bake for 5 minutes or until toasty. Spread a small amount of chilli jam over each slice. Cover with goats cheese, spreading smoothly with a palette knife. Evenly top with tomatoes, sprinkle with sea salt and black pepper.

Optional: Garnish with a lovely fresh basil leaf.

Grilled Haloumi

SERVES 4

- *200g haloumi cheese*
- *3 tbs. plain flour*
- *3 tbs. (45ml) olive oil*

Cut haloumi into eight slices. Season the flour with sea salt and pepper and roll haloumi in it coating both sides well. Heat oil in a non-stick frying pan until hot and add haloumi. Fry three pieces for 1–2 minutes on each side or until golden brown. Remove, drain and lay on a serving plate.

Optional: Garnish with sprigs of parsley and serve with hot pita bread. This is also delicious served drizzled with Caramalised Balsamic Vinegar (see: Salad Dressings) and Tomato Salsa (see: Sauces, Salsas & Marinades).

Lebanese Crisps

SERVES 6

Recipe by Jeff Thode.

- *1 pkt of Lebanese flat bread*
- *⅓ cup (85ml) olive oil*
- *4 gloves garlic, crushed*

Preheat oven to 180°C. Spread the bread with olive oil and garlic, cut into sixteenths before baking until golden brown. Sprinkle with salt. Bread will crisp further when cool.

Marinated Olives

SERVES 4

- *300g mixed olives (black and green)*
- *1 lemon, juice and zest*
- *2 tbs. fresh thyme leaves*
- *½ cup (125ml) olive oil*

Pop first three ingredients into a sealable jar. Pour oil into a small saucepan. Heat over medium-low heat until just warm. Pour over olives. Seal. Turn jars upside down and stand for 5 minutes. Turn upright. Allow to infuse for 1 week, turning once daily. These olives will keep for up to 1 month in the fridge.

Tip: The only difference between green olives and black olives is ripeness. Being riper, black olives contain more oil than green.

Olive Tapenade Palmiers

MAKES 48

- *2 sheets butter puff pastry*
- *½ cup olive tapenade*
- *¼ cup parmesan grated cheese*

Preheat oven 220°C. Line a baking tray with baking paper. Place pastry on a clean working surface. Spread with tapenade. Top with parmesan cheese. Fold 2 opposite sides of 1 pastry sheet into the centre. Fold in half to form a double log and repeat with remaining pastry. Chill in freezer for 5 minutes. Remove and cut into 1cm thick pieces. Place on trays and cook for 25–30 minutes or until puffed and golden.

Optional: Substitute olive tapenade with sun dried tomato pesto and fresh basil leaves.

Prawn & Fruit Kebabs

MAKES 10

Recipe from Janelle McCosker.

- *20 cooked prawns, peeled and deveined*
- *½ fresh pineapple, cut into chunks*
- *¼ watermelon, cubed*
- *½ rockmelon, cubed*

Thread the prawns and fruit onto skewers. Chill covered for 5–10 minutes before serving. This is a light, refreshing appetiser.

Roasted Pears with Blue Cheese

SERVES 4

- *1 pear, peeled, halved and cored*
- *45g mild blue cheese*
- *100g pkt fresh salad leaves*
- *2 tbs. (30ml) balsamic vinegar*

Preheat oven 200°C and line a baking tray with baking paper. Place each pear half on the paper and crumble blue cheese over the top. Bake in the oven for 8 minutes. Distribute salad leaves evenly over 4 plates, pop the warm pears on top and drizzle with balsamic vinegar.

Optional: Serve with crusty rye bread.

Savoury Celery Sticks

SERVES 4–6

- *½ bunch celery sticks*
- *125g cream cheese*
- *2 whole finely chopped gherkins*
- *¼ red onion, finely diced*

Wash celery sticks and cut into 6cm lengths. Beat cheese in a bowl until smooth. Stir in gherkin and onion. Mix well. Season to taste with salt and pepper. Fill celery with cream cheese mixture.

Tip: If celery does not sit or rolls to one side, simply peel a layer or two off the celery base with a potato peeler to flatten.

Semi-Dried Tomato Pesto

- *100g semi-dried tomatoes*
- *3 tbs. (45ml) olive oil*
- *1 tbs. tomato paste*
- *2 tbs. pine nuts (or macadamia nuts)*

Process all ingredients in a food processor until desired texture is reached.

Hint: Pesto can be added to soups, stews, dressings and sandwiches to tantalise tastebuds. This can be stored in the fridge for up to a week or freeze and defrost as needed.

Stuffed Cucumbers

SERVES 6

- *3 cucumbers, peeled*
- *125g cream cheese, softened*
- *¼ cup stuffed green olives, chopped*
- *6 chive stalks*

Cut cucumbers in half lengthwise, scoop out centres. Beat cheese until creamy, add olives and chives, season. Fill centre of cucumber with cheese mixture. Press halves together, wrap tightly in cling wrap and chill. Slice crosswise in thick slices to serve.

Tandoori Chicken Cucumber Basket

MAKES 30

A recipe from Chef Laurent Vancam.

- *2 continental cucumbers, top 'n' tailed*
- *100g poached free range chicken breast, chopped*
- *2 tbs. natural yoghurt*
- *2 tbs. tandoori paste*

Cut cucumber lengthways in half and then into 15 pieces approx. 1.5cm long. Scoop out the centre to make a basket for the filling. Mix chicken with yoghurt and tandoori paste. Place 1 tsp. of the mixture into each basket and serve chilled.

Optional: If you have mint, chop a little into the mix for a refreshing flavour. Also delicious served with prawn or crab meat and sweet chilli with ginger sauce and freshly chopped coriander.

Thai Chicken Meatballs

SERVES 6–8

Recipe from Lisa Elliot ... These are FANTASTIC!

- *500g free range chicken mince*
- *¼ cup (62ml) sweet chilli sauce, plus extra for dipping*
- *3 spring onions, chopped*
- *1 bunch coriander, chopped*

Preheat oven 180°C. Combine ingredients in a bowl, season and with wet hands shape into meatballs. Place on a paper-lined baking tray and bake for 15–20 minutes.

Optional: Serve with extra sweet chilli sauce or Dipping Sauce (see: Sauces, Salsas & Marinades).

Light Meals & Lunches

One day your life will flash before your eyes. Make sure it's worth watching!

Author Unknown

Soups

Artichoke & Garlic Soup

SERVES 4–6

- *3 tbs. (45g) butter*
- *6 fresh artichoke hearts*
- *3 cloves garlic, thinly sliced*
- *1 ltr. vegetable stock*

Heat butter over medium heat and sauté the artichoke hearts and garlic until golden. Add stock and bring to a boil. Lower heat and simmer for 10 minutes or until the artichoke is tender. Blend until smooth. Season to taste.

Tip: Artichokes are a fabulous source of fibre, vitamin C, magnesium and potassium. To cook with just artichoke hearts, remove all the tough outer leaves. Stop removing leaves when you get to the tender, light green ones that form the heart.

Broccoli Soup

SERVES 2

- *2 broccoli heads, cut into florets and stalks shredded*
- *2 cloves garlic, crushed*
- *2 cups chicken stock*
- *½ cup cream*

Mix broccoli, garlic and chicken stock in a saucepan, cook until broccoli softens. Season with salt and pepper and add cream. Blend until smooth. *Delicious!*

Carrot & Ginger Soup

SERVES 4

This is the inspirational Louise L. Hay's favourite soup.

- *2 spring onions, sliced*
- *1 tbs. freshly grated ginger*
- *12 medium carrots, peeled and sliced*
- *1 ltr. vegetable or chicken stock*

In a large saucepan, sauté the green onions and ginger for about 5 minutes. Add the carrots and sauté for a few more minutes. Add the stock and bring to a boil. Turn heat to low and simmer for 30 minutes or until carrots are tender. Transfer soup to a blender or food processor and purée until smooth.

Optional: Season with sea salt and pepper, cumin and lemon juice to taste. For something really different, add a cup of orange juice and only 3 cups of stock ... Yummy!

Tip: This soup can be made in larger batches and frozen ready for a quick snack at any time.

Chapattis

SERVES 4

- *2 cups (350g) plain flour*
- *1 tsp. ghee*
- *1 tsp. salt*

Mix all the ingredients together with an adequate amount of water to knead into a smooth dough (start with ½ cup and increase to 1). Leave for an hour. Tear into equal size portions and knead into balls. Cover with dry flour, roll out on a flat, floured surface. Heat a grill and pop chapatti onto it. Moderately roast both sides until nice and toasted.

Optional: Serve with any soups, curries or dips.

Coconut & Pea Soup

SERVES 4

- *2 spring onions, chopped*
- *1 tsp. finely grated ginger*
- *2 x 400ml cans coconut milk*
- *500g green peas*

In a large non stick saucepan sauté onions and ginger in a little water until tender. Add coconut milk and bring to a boil. Stir in the peas and bring to the boil again. Remove from heat and allow to cool. Puree in a blender until smooth. Season to taste. Add more fresh ginger to the soup if desired.

Greek Lemon Soup

SERVES 4

A recipe from Victoria Nacson who calls it "Liquid Penicillin."

- *1 ltr. organic chicken stock*
- *4 cloves garlic, crushed*
- *1 free range egg*
- *1 lemon, juiced*

Bring the stock to the boil. Add the garlic and then turn the heat off. In a bowl beat the egg vigorously and slowly add the juice to it. It's very important that you don't stop beating or the egg will curdle. Keep beating, add a ladle of stock until the bowl is full. Stir the soup in the saucepan and slowly mix in the egg mixture from the bowl. Do not stop stirring or you will end up with scrambled egg soup. This soup is delicious and very therapeutic.

Optional: Season with pepper and some grated lemon rind. You can add a half cup of cooked rice when you add the garlic too.

Green Pea & Chicken Soup

SERVES 4

- *2 free range chicken carcasses*
- *2 brown onions, chopped*
- *2 carrots, peeled and chopped*
- *500g fresh green peas*

Preheat oven 200°C. Place chicken on a baking tray and bake for an hour. Remove and place in medium pot with just enough water to cover. Add onion and carrots bring boil and simmer for 3 hours. Add more water if reducing, add peas and simmer until peas are soft. Remove carcass, pick off any excess meat, season and puree.

Laksa

SERVES 4

- *200g bean vermicelli noodles*
- *3 tbs. Laksa paste*
- *400ml can coconut milk*
- *12 green prawns, peeled and deveined*

Soak vermicelli in hot water until soft, drain and set aside. Into a saucepan add paste, heat until fragrant then add coconut milk and 1 cup of water. Bring to the boil. Add prawns and noodles, reduce heat and simmer for 3–5 minutes just enough to heat the prawns. Serve warm.

Optional: Add a selection of vegetables to this if you have them ...
Snow peas, bean shoots, baby corn, carrot, spring onions,
bok choy ... Whatever your family will eat!

Leek & Potato Soup

SERVES 4

- *4 cups sliced leek, white stems only*
- *3 cups of peeled and chopped potatoes*
- *5 cups (1.25ltr) chicken stock*
- *¼ cup crème fraiche*

In a large saucepan, add leeks, potato and stock (make your own for a bigger, richer flavour). Bring to the boil, cover, reduce heat and simmer until vegetables are soft. This will take about 20 minutes. Puree this mixture and return to the pan. Stir in the creme fraiche, season with sea salt and pepper to taste.

Optional: For a richer flavour if serving immediately, sweat the leeks
in butter first before adding the potato and stock.

Lentil & Carrot Soup

SERVES 4–6

A recipe from Donna McCosker.

- *½ cup (85g) lentils, rinsed*
- *1 ltr. chicken stock*
- *2 carrots, sliced*

Combine all ingredients in a large saucepan and bring to the boil. Simmer for 15 minutes or until the lentils have swollen and softened. Blend and season before serving.

Optional: Serve with a dollop of yoghurt and sprinkled with toasted cumin seeds.

Poached Chicken in Pea Broth

SERVES 4

This is magic, TRY IT!

- *2 cups (500ml) chicken stock*
- *4 free range chicken breasts, sliced*
- *1 brown onion, diced*
- *3 cups green peas*

In a non-stick frying pan add stock, chicken and onion then bring to boil. Simmer till chicken is cooked through. Add peas, season with cracked black pepper and salt and simmer for 5 more minutes.

Optional: Serve sprinkled with fresh, flavoursome thyme leaves if you have them.

Roasted Tomato Basil Soup

SERVES 4

- *12 Roma tomatoes, chopped*
- *2 red onions, chopped*
- *5 tbs. tomato paste*
- *3 tbs. basil pesto*

Preheat oven 200°C. Place tomatoes and onions on a baking paper lined tray and coat evenly with the tomato paste. Bake for 30 minutes. Place in a food processor and blend. Add basil pesto. Add hot, salted water to reduce thickness until you reach your desired consistency. Season with cracked black pepper to serve.

Spinach Soup

SERVES 2–4

- *3 cups (750ml) vegetable stock*
- *1 bunch silverbeet*
- *1 large onion, chopped*
- *2 medium potatoes, peeled and chopped*

Get the stock simmering nicely, wash and shred the silverbeet removing any tough stalks, add it with onion and potatoes to the stock. Season lightly. Let simmer for 15 minutes or until the vegetables are softened. Blend and serve immediately.

Optional: Fresh nutmeg goes particularly well with spinach, so if you have it grate to garnish.

Thyme, Leek & Asparagus Soup

SERVES 4

- *1 potato, peeled and diced*
- *1 leek, remove top green leaves, and roughly chop*
- *250g fresh asparagus, snap off woody ends and cut*
- *3 sprigs of thyme, leaves removed*

Place 2 cups (500ml) water in a saucepan, add potato, leek and leaves from two thyme sprigs. Cover and simmer for 15 minutes or until soft. Return to a rapid boil. Add asparagus and boil for 5 minutes, puree, season to taste and serve sprinkled with remaining thyme.

Optional: Swirl through a little crème fraiche for a pretty presentation.

Tomato & Thyme Soup

SERVES 4

Recipe from Michelle Dodd.

- *16 Roma tomatoes*
- *2 tbs. garlic infused olive oil*
- *4 sprigs fresh thyme, leaves removed*
- *1 ltr. vegetable stock*

Preheat oven 180°C. Slice tomatoes in half, place onto a foil lined baking tray with the cut side up and drizzle with oil. Season with sea salt, pepper and thyme leaves. Bake for 30–40 minutes. Remove and allow to cool slightly. Blend tomatoes and pour into a saucepan, add stock and simmer for 15 minutes. Serve warm with fresh, crusty bread.

All Others

The big secret in life is that there is no big secret.
Whatever your goal, you can get there if you're willing to work.

Oprah Winfrey

Asian Chicken Wraps

MAKES 2

- *1 cup of leftover roast chicken meat*
- *1–2 tbs. teriyaki sauce*
- *¼ Chinese cabbage, finely shredded*
- *2 wholemeal wraps*

Over a low heat, gently warm chicken meat and teriyaki sauce. Remove and cool. Spread mix over wraps and top with cabbage. Roll, cut in half and enjoy!

Optional: Add some red pepper flakes and freshly grated ginger to the teriyaki sauce for a burst of Asian flavour.

Balsamic Chicken & Avocado Salad

SERVES 4

- *1 cup (250ml) caramelised balsamic vinegar*
- *4 free range chicken breasts, sliced*
- *4 Roma tomatoes, quartered*
- *3 avocados, quartered*

In a bowl mix ½ cup balsamic vinegar with the chicken and marinate for 1 hour. In a non-stick frying pan, cook chicken for 4–5 minutes, turning once. Remove from heat and cool. Place in a mixing bowl, add tomatoes and avocado and season. Gently toss. Drizzle with balsamic vinegar before serving.

Chicken Walnut Salad

SERVES 4

- *½ cup (125ml) red wine vinegar*
- *2 free range chicken breasts, sliced*
- *2 cup walnuts, toasted*
- *120g baby spinach*

In a non-stick frying pan heat vinegar, add sliced chicken and poach till cooked. Set aside. When cool, mix all ingredients together and season before serving drizzled with remaining jus.

Chilli Tuna

SERVES 4

Recipe from Lauren Sproat.

- *2 cups boiled rice (white or brown)*
- *220g can tuna in freshwater*
- *2 tbs. natural yoghurt*
- *4 tbs. (60ml) sweet chilli sauce*

Stir tuna through rice, combine yoghurt and sweet chilli sauce and mix through the rice. Chill until ready to serve with a lovely green salad for lunch ... *This is yummy!*

Crab Cakes

MAKES 4

- 2 cups white crab meat, squeezed of excess water
- 20g piece fresh ginger, peeled and grated
- ½ tbs. korma curry paste
- ½ cup freshly chopped coriander

Mix altogether and shape into patties. Cook in a non-stick frying pan for 3 minutes each side or until golden brown.

Optional: Serve with Lime Mayonnaise (see: Sauce, Salsas & Marinades).

Deepak's Favourite Snack

SERVES 1

- 1 hard boiled egg
- A pinch of curry powder
- 1 leaf of cos lettuce
- 1 pita bread

Lay the pita bread out on a dish. Place the cos lettuce in the middle of the bread. Peel the hard boiled egg, place in a bowl, mash the egg with a fork and then mix in the curry powder. Place the curried egg mixture on the lettuce and roll it up. A great snack that can be enjoyed anytime of the day.

Grilled Parmesan Polenta

SERVES 4 OR 8 AS A SIDE.

- *2 cups (500ml) milk*
- *2 cups (500ml) chicken stock*
- *1 cup instant polenta*
- *½ cup grated parmesan cheese*

Line a loaf tin with baking paper. Bring milk and stock to the boil in a saucepan over medium heat. Pour in polenta in a steady stream, whisking constantly. Cook, stirring, for 5 minutes or until thick. Season with salt and pepper. Stir in parmesan. Spoon into dish. Smooth surface. Refrigerate for 3 hours or until firm. Preheat BBQ grill on medium-high heat. Turn polenta out. Slice into 2cm thick pieces. Cook for 2 minutes each side or until golden. Serve warm.

Optional: Depending on the state of your grill, you may need to oil polenta fingers before barbequing . Very tasty served topped with a fresh Tomato Salsa (See: Sauces, Salsas & Marinades).

Garlic Prawns

SERVES 1

- *6 green prawns*
- *4 cloves garlic, crushed*
- *1 small chilli, halved with seeds removed*
- *3 tbs. (45g) butter*

Preheat oven 190°C. Shell prawns, leaving the tails on. Combine garlic, chilli and butter. Pour into a shallow oven proof dish, add prawns and cook for 6 minutes or until sizzling.

Optional: Can be grilled on a BBQ as well and are delicious served atop a cold noodle salad.

Indian Chickpea & Potato Patties

SERVES 4

- *300g can chickpeas*
- *2 cups leftover mashed potato*
- *3 tbs. Gourmet Garden Indian blend*
- *½ cup freshly cut coriander*

Pulse chickpeas in a food processor until roughly chopped. Transfer to a bowl. Add remaining ingredients. Season with pepper and stir until combined. Using a ¼ cup measure shape mixture into 12 patties. Cook in a non-stick frying pan over medium heat for 3–4 minutes on each side or until golden.

Light Wrap

SERVES 4

Recipe from Wayne Dyer.

- *1 can chickpeas, rinsed and drained*
- *2 wholemeal wraps*
- *½ small ripe avocado, peeled*
- *6 rocket leaves, washed and dried*

The kids and I love this and I've got eight of them! Place chickpeas in a food processor and process until smooth. Lay the wholemeal wrap on a plate and spread evenly with chickpea paste, top with rocket and avocado. Roll up and enclose filling. Cut in half diagonally and serve immediately.

Mozzarella & Tomato Pasta Bake

SERVES 4

- 400g cooked penne, cooked
- 4 tbs. olive tapenade
- 1 cup semi dried tomatoes with oil
- 1 cup grated mozzarella cheese

Preheat oven to 180°C. Mix together first three ingredients and ½ the cheese, season with cracked black pepper. Pour into a baking dish and top with remaining cheese. Bake in oven for 15 minutes or until cheese is golden brown.

Optional: Serve with a light green salad drizzled with balsamic vinaigrette.

Pea & Mint Frittata

SERVES 2–4

- 1 tsp. butter
- 4 free range eggs, beaten
- ½ cup (50g) fresh peas
- 2 tbs. freshly chopped mint

Heat butter in a non-stick frying pan. Add peas and sauté for 1 minute. Season eggs with sea salt, pepper and mint before pouring into the pan. Reduce heat to low and cook for 5 minutes or until the base is set. Place the frittata under a medium preheated grill (ensure your frying pan has a metal handle) for 4–5 minutes or until cooked through. Allow to cool slightly then cut into wedges.

Optional: This is delicious served with a fresh green salad.

Potato & Pea Samosas

MAKES 8

- *4 potatoes, cut into cubes*
- *1 cup peas*
- *200g tikka masala sauce*
- *2 sheets butter puff pastry*

Preheat oven 180°C. In a pot of boiling water, cook potatoes for 5–6 minutes or until tender. Drain and cool. Put potatoes, peas and tikka masala sauce in a non-stick frying pan and simmer for 10 minutes. Cut pastry into quarters, place filling in centre of each square. Fold pastry over into a triangle shape and press edges with fork. Trim to neaten and bake for 15 minutes.

Optional: For a sensational lunch serve with Minted Yoghurt (see: Sauces, Salsas & Marinades).

Pepper Crusted Chicken

SERVES 4

D.e.l.i.c.i.o.u.s!

- *2 cups bread crumbs*
- *2 free range eggs, whisked*
- *12 free range chicken tenderloins*
- *½ cup (125ml) olive oil*

Add a tsp. of cracked black pepper to bread crumbs. Roll chicken in eggs, then coat in breadcrumbs. Place onto a paper lined baking tray and chill in the fridge for 10 minutes. Heat oil in a non-stick frying pan to hot and fry chicken for 3 minutes each side or until golden brown.

Optional: Delicious served with Tomato & Honey Salsa (see: Sauces, Salsas & Marinades) and a fresh green salad.

Rosemary Chicken Skewers

MAKES 12

These will impress your guests.

- *4 free range chicken breasts*
- *12 sprigs rosemary (with leaves and stalks)*
- *1 tbs. honey*
- *1 lemon, zest and juice*

Gently beat chicken until 1 cm thick. Cut each breast into 3 or 4 strips and place on a tray. Remove the leaves from the rosemary sprigs leaving a few at the top and soak the stems in cold water. Chop removed leaves and transfer to a bowl with the honey, lemon juice and zest and season. Pour over chicken, cover and chill for at least 1 hour. Thread a piece of chicken onto each rosemary stalk. Heat a grill and cook for 5–6 minutes or until cooked through.

Optional: These are lovely drizzled with a little Honey Lemon Dressing (see: Salad Dressings).

Salmon & Cream Cheese Bagel

SERVES 1

- *1 plain bagel*
- *1 slice of thinly sliced smoked salmon*
- *1–2 tbs. chive cream cheese*
- *½ tsp. drained capers*

Slice the bagel in half and spread the cream cheese on the cut sides. Top with sliced salmon and sprinkle with capers. Season with cracked black pepper. Top with the remaining half of the bagel and lightly press. Enjoy!

Optional: Substitute capers for cucumber.

Salmon Ceviche

SERVES 4

- *2 x 250g salmon fillets*
- *2 lemons, juiced*
- *¼ cup (62ml) mirin*
- *2 tbs. freshly chopped dill*

On a baking tray lay enough cling film to cover it. Place the salmon fillets on it and pop into the freezer for 10 minutes. Remove and slice the salmon thinly. Arrange on a serving platter overlapping the slices ever so slightly. For the dressing, whisk remaining ingredients with the zest of 1 lemon, season with sea salt and pepper. Pour over salmon, cover and refrigerate for 4 hours.

Tip: 'Ceviche' is a method of cooking where you basically marinate the raw fish in highly acidic citrus juice.

Optional: Serve with a light, green salad or mixed cress if in season.

San Choy Bow

SERVES 4

- *8 iceberg lettuce leaves*
- *500g free range chicken mince*
- *125g can water chestnuts, drained*
- *3–4 tbs. oyster sauce*

Trim lettuce leaves and cover in cold water, soak in refrigerator for 15 minutes then drain. Heat a wok over high heat. Add chicken mince and fry for 2–3 minutes, breaking up any lumps with a wooden spoon. Add sliced water chestnuts and oyster sauce and stir-fry for a further 2–3 minutes. To serve, spoon filling into lettuce leaves, roll up and enjoy!

Stuffed Tomato with Couscous

MAKES 6

- 6 vine-ripe tomatoes, (leave stem on for presentation)
- 1 jar of marinated capsicums
- 6 tbs. fresh basil
- 4 cups pearl couscous

Preheat oven 180°C. Cut the top of the tomatoes reserving the lid. Scoop out the inside setting the flesh aside. Place the tomatoes (and lids) on a baking tray and bake for 10 minutes. Meanwhile, chop tomato flesh and add to a bowl with the capsicum and oil from the jar. Mix through basil. Bring four cups of water and couscous to the boil. Remove from heat and cover. Steam for 10 minutes. Remove tomatoes from oven and allow to cool. Mix couscous through tomato and capsicum and season. Spoon mixture into tomato shells, replace lids and serve.

Tomato, Haloumi & Watercress Salad

SERVES 6

- 2 tbs. (30ml) garlic infused olive oil
- 200g haloumi cheese, sliced
- 6 roma tomatoes, sliced
- ½ bunch watercress

In a non-stick frying pan heat half the oil and grill each slice of cheese 1–2 minutes each side or until golden brown. Arrange tomatoes on a long, white serving plate, set cheese on top, season with sea salt and cracked black pepper. Garnish with watercress and drizzle with remaining oil.

Optional: Drizzle with some lemon juice, its sourness is a nice balance for the saltiness of the haloumi.

Sushi

MAKES 6

- *1¼ cups short grain rice*
- *¼ cup (60ml) rice vinegar*
- *1 tbs. organic raw sugar*
- *1 pkt nori/seaweed sheets*

Rinse rice under running water until water runs clear, drain well. Place in saucepan with 1½ cups water (375ml) simmer for 20–25 minutes or until tender. Cover for 15 minutes. Combine the vinegar, sugar and 1 tsp. salt. Stir until sugar dissolves, place rice in a bowl and pour the rice vinegar on top. Mix gently with a spatula and allow to cool to room temperature. Place a nori sheet onto bamboo mat, shiny side down, spread rice 1cm thick over sheet leaving a 1cm border. Wet hands slightly and line with filling of choice, then roll gently (but firmly) using a bamboo mat to create a compacted roll. Remove from mat, wet a sharp knife and cut into 2cm slices, chill before serving.

Optional: For that authentic Japanese flavour serve with light soy sauce, wasabi and pickled ginger, sensational, fresh and healthy!

Filling Ideas:

- *Cucumber, egg, avocado, wasabi mayonnaise*
- *Tuna, avocado, chives, mayonnaise*
- *Smoked salmon, cream cheese, cucumber, dill*
- *Teriyaki chicken, cucumber, capsicum*
- *Tofu teriyaki, egg, cucumber*

Tip: You can buy a delicious Japanese mayonnaise in all Asian sections of most supermarkets.

Sides

It's important to honour and respect the path others are on.

Deepak Chopra

Salads

Avocado Stuffed Eggs

MAKES 12

- *½ dozen eggs, hard boiled*
- *½ avocado, cubed*
- *1 tbs. (15ml) lemon juice*
- *2 tbs. organic mayonnaise*

Slice the eggs in half lengthwise and carefully remove the yolks from the egg whites and place into a bowl with the avocado, lemon juice and mayonnaise, season with sea salt and pepper. Gently mash with a fork. Spoon the yolk mixture back into the egg white cases, cover and chill prior to serving.

Optional: Sprinkle with paprika for flavour and presentation.

Tip: How to boil the perfect egg … Place eggs in a saucepan, cover with cold water (do not salt) and, on high heat, bring to the boil. Reduce heat immediately and gently boil, uncovered, for 1 minute per egg for a soft-boiled egg, 2 minutes per egg for a medium-boiled egg, and 3 minutes per egg for a hard-boiled egg.

Artichoke Salad

SERVES 4–6

Recipe from Biance Aiono.

- *250g fresh green beans, trimmed*
- *1 jar marinated artichoke hearts, drained (reserving 2 tbs. oil for dressing)*
- *½ cup unsalted pistachios, chopped*
- *4 flat leaf parsley stems, chopped*

Cook green beans in boiling salted water uncovered for 3–4 minutes. Drain. Coarsely chop artichoke hearts. Combine all ingredients in medium bowl and toss gently to coat.

Optional: Delicious serve drizzled with reserved oil and 1 tbs. balsamic vinegar. As a general rule a Balsamic Vinaigrette is made 2 parts oil: 1 part balsamic.

Bang Bang Chicken Salad

SERVES 4

A recipe from Suzanne Bradley that is a weekly staple ... It's scrummy!

- *120g mixed salad*
- *2 free range chicken breasts, sliced*
- *¼ cup (62ml) sesame oil*
- *½ cup (130g) crunchy peanut butter*

Place salad on a long rectangular serving plate. Grill the chicken in the hot sesame oil for 2–3 minutes each side or until tender. Remove from heat and rest to cool before laying on top of the salad. Microwave peanut butter with 2 tbs. of water stirring every 30 seconds until runny. Drizzle over chicken and salad.

Optional: Can use Chinese cabbage, finely shredded and a variety of freshly chopped vegetables for extra texture and colour.

Broad Bean Salad

SERVES 6

- *400g broad beans, peeled*
- *½ cup shaved pecorino*
- *3 tbs. (45ml) extra virgin olive oil*
- *6 tbs. fresh mint*

Place all ingredients in a bowl. Mix and season with cracked black pepper and salt.

Optional: If you have a lemon, you could add some lemon juice for a little zing. If fresh broad beans are unavailable, buy frozen.

Caramelised Pear & Rocket Salad

SERVES 6

- *6 pears, sliced*
- *200g baby rocket salad mix*
- *8 tbs. freshly grated parmesan*
- *3 tbs. (45ml) balsamic vinegar*

In a non-stick frying pan over a medium heat, add sliced pear. The natural juices of the pear will release, cook till soft and slightly browned. Set aside and cool. In a bowl place the rocket and sprinkle with parmesan. Top with warm pear and serve drizzled with balsamic vinegar.

Tip: Use varieties of pears that remain firm when cooking it like Bartlett, Bosc or Packhams. Firm pears have a long storage life and ripen best after they are harvested. Pears are one of the few fruits that do not ripen successfully on the tree.

Cauliflower & Sesame Seed Salad

SERVES 4–6

A recipe by Robin Brown ... Soooo simple and soooo enjoyable!

- *2–3 tbs. sesame seeds*
- *½ raw cauliflower, broken into florets*
- *2 tbs. egg mayonnaise*

Toast sesame seeds over a dry heat for 2 minutes or until golden. Use enough mayonnaise to coat the cauliflower and half of the sesame seeds. Toss until the cauliflower is well coated. Chill and serve sprinkled with the remaining sesame seeds.

Cherry Bomb Salad

SERVES 6

A recipe from Dan Primmer.

- *50g kalamata olives, marinated in olive oil*
- *2 zucchinis, diced*
- *2 punnets cherry tomatoes*
- *½ cup fresh oregano*

Heat 4 tbs. of olive oil from the olives in a non-stick frying pan over medium/high heat, add olives then zucchini. Sauté for 2 minutes. Add tomatoes then oregano, continue to sauté until zucchinis are golden and tomatoes are soft. Season with cracked black pepper and serve.

Hint: This salad is delicious served with grilled chicken or fish or Grilled Parmesan Polenta (see: Light Lunches).

Coconut Salad

SERVES 4

Yum Scrum!

- 2 cups shaved coconut, toasted
- 3 cups peeled and diced sweet potato (kumara), roasted
- 2 cups diced pumpkin, roasted
- ½ cup fresh coriander

Mix all ingredients in a serving bowl, season with sea salt and pepper and serve.

Crisp Eggplant Salad

SERVES 4–6

- 1 fresh eggplant, thinly sliced
- 150g marinated fetta with oil, crumbled
- 1 cos lettuce, halved
- 4 stems of basil leaves, torn

Brush eggplant with 1 tbs. of oil from the fetta. Place in a frying pan over medium/high heat and cook for 2–3 minutes on each side or until crisp and golden. Place lettuce leaves on serving plates and top with eggplant slices, fetta, basil and season. Drizzle with a little of the fetta oil before serving.

Hint: Eggplants are best used as soon as bought, as left in the fridge they tend to brown and turn bitter when cooked.

Green Salad

SERVES 4–6

- *120g mixed lettuce*
- *1 cup snow peas*
- *2 Lebanese cucumbers*
- *1 avocado, flesh removed and cut into chunks*

Wash and dry the lettuce, snow peas and cucumber. Slice the cucumber (peel it first if you like). Put all ingredients into a bowl, and stir gently to mix. Serve with dressing of your choice (goes nicely with vinaigrette).

Optional: Can add 3 finely sliced spring onions or ½ cup fresh herbs (e.g. parsley or coriander) if in your fridge.

Mango Salad

SERVES 4

Recipe from Jacqui Burnie.

- *120g English spinach leaves*
- *1 avocado, sliced*
- *1 large, ripe mango, sliced*
- *½ cup macadamia halves, lightly toasted*

Place salad in a serving bowl. Gently toss through remaining ingredients.

Optional: Dress with a dollop of the delicious Mango Mayonnaise (see: Sauces, Salsas & Marinades).

Mango Chickpea Salad

SERVES 4

This is marvelous!

- *400g can chickpeas*
- *2 mangoes, chopped*
- *4 tbs. coriander, chopped*
- *2 limes, squeezed*

Combine all ingredients, season and serve.

Marinated Field Mushroom Salad

SERVES 4

These are beautiful, the flavour and texture simply divine.

- *⅓ cup (85ml) balsamic vinegar*
- *4 cloves garlic, crushed*
- *8 tbs. fresh oregano*
- *10 large field mushrooms*

In a large bowl, mix the first three ingredients together, season with sea salt and cracked pepper. Add mushrooms and completely coat with sauce. Cover the bowl with cling film and marinate for at least 30 minutes. Remove cling film and place mushrooms on a paper lined baking tray, bake in a 180°C oven for 20 minutes. Serve warm or cool as a side or salad.

Tip: Blueberries contain more antioxidants than any other fruit, but oregano ranks even higher. So lots of fresh oregano in this salad make it a very healthy one!

Orange & Carrot Salad

SERVES 4

- *1 carrot, grated*
- *1 orange, peeled, segmented and chopped (reserve juice)*
- *2 tbs. shredded coconut, toasted*
- *2 tbs. sultanas*

Combine all the ingredients in a bowl and toss together. Drizzle with the orange juice, as it provides a natural, healthy dressing.

Papaya & Pineapple Salad

SERVES 4–6

- *1 small pineapple, peeled*
- *1 red papaya, peeled*
- *1 red chilli, chopped*
- *1 tbs. (15ml) rice wine vinegar*

Use a sharp knife to remove the eyes from pineapple, then cut pineapple into paper thin slices. Cut papaya into quarters, remove seeds and slice thinly. Arrange fruits on a flat serving plate. Combine chilli and vinegar and drizzle over. Served chilled.

Hint: Papaya, also known as 'Paw Paw' is a very effective fruit aiding digestion.

Pomegranate & Apple Salad

SERVES 4

- ¾ cup of pomegranate seeds
- 1 Fuji apple, cut into pieces
- 2 tsp. lemon juice
- 1 tsp. honey

Toss all ingredients together and serve chilled.

Optional: Add some freshly chopped mint if you have it growing in your garden.

Hint: Pomegranates keep for up to a month in the fridge. To deseed one, cut 2cm off the top of the fruit (be careful as the juice may stain your clothing). Score the pomegranate skin from the top to the base so that you have 5 evenly spaced cuts. While holding the pomegranate underwater, pull the fruit apart. The pomegranate seeds (arils) will sink to the bottom and any membrane or pith will float to the top of the water.

Pumpkin & Pepitas Salad

SERVES 4

- 400g pumpkin, peeled, chopped and roasted
- ¼ cup pepitas
- ⅓ cup sour cream
- 1 tsp. ground cumin

Pop pumpkin and pepitas into a serving bowl. Mix cream and cumin together and use to dress the pumpkin and pepitas.

Optional: Add a splash of lemon juice to the dressing. Also nice with avocado if you have some in your fridge. Serve sprinkled with a few extra pepitas.

Radish with Honey & Mustard

SERVES 4

- *1 tsp. balsamic vinegar*
- *1 tsp. honey*
- *1 tsp. mustard*
- *½ cup sliced radish*

Mix vinegar, honey and mustard with a pinch of sea salt. Arrange radish slices on a plate and drizzle with dressing.

Hint: Radishes are a great detox food especially for the liver.

Roast Beetroot & Fetta Salad

SERVES 4

- *5 beetroots, peeled and cut into quarters*
- *200g fetta, cubed*
- *½ cup shredded mint*
- *1 cup walnuts, toasted and chopped*

Preheat oven 180°C. Place beetroots on a baking tray and season with salt and pepper. Cover with foil and bake for 40-45 minutes or until tender. Remove from tray and cool. Place in a serving dish and gently toss through fetta, mint and walnuts.

Optional: This is lovely drizzled with Lemon Mustard Vinaigrette (see: Salad Dressings).

Roasted Tomatoes

SERVES 4–6

- *1kg vine-ripened cherry tomatoes*
- *2 tbs. (30ml) olive oil*
- *2 tbs. (30ml) balsamic vinegar*

Preheat oven 220°C. Line a baking tray with baking paper, pop tomatoes on the tray and drizzle with oil and vinegar. Season with ground pepper and roast for about 15 minutes or until tomatoes just start to collapse.

Optional: Serve these as a side with polenta cakes, omelettes or frittatas or on top of English Spinach for a lovely Roasted Tomato Salad.

Rocket Salad

SERVES 4–6

- *100g rocket*
- *¼ cup pine nuts, toasted*
- *⅓ cup (85ml) balsamic vinegar*
- *¼ cup parmesan cheese, thinly sliced or grated*

Wash and dry rocket. Place in salad bowl with pine nuts and toss with the balsamic dressing. Sprinkle with parmesan cheese and gently mix.

Sesame Cucumber Ribbons

SERVES 4

- *2 Lebanese cucumbers*
- *2 tsp. sesame seeds*
- *½ chilli, deseeded and finely chopped*
- *1 lemon*

Using a vegie peeler, slice cucumbers into long thin ribbons. Place in a bowl, sprinkle with sesame seeds, chilli and toss to coat. Drizzle with lemon juice.

Optional: This is delicious served with nearly all fish and legume based patties.

Spinach & Apple Salad

SERVES 4

- *2 cloves garlic, unpeeled*
- *2 slices wholemeal bread, crusts removed*
- *100g baby spinach leaves*
- *2 crisp, red-skinned apples, cored and sliced*

Roast garlic cloves under a hot grill for 4 minutes or until blackened. When cooled, squeeze out the garlic flesh and mash. Spread one side of the bread slices with the garlic paste, then dice. Arrange on a baking tray and grill for 1–2 minutes, turning from time to time until brown. Toss the spinach and apple together in a serving bowl, and scatter with croutons. Season with sea salt and pepper.

Optional: Add some artichokes or walnuts. Herb Dressing compliments this salad beautifully (see: Salad Dressings).

Smoked Salmon & Watercress Salad

SERVES 4

Great for a summer BBQ or light lunch.

- *6 tbs. baby capers*
- *6 tbs. garlic infused olive oil*
- *8 slices smoked salmon*
- *1 bunch baby watercress*

Drain capers from jar and reserve juice. Place juice in a bowl with olive oil. On a nice white platter, arrange salmon so as not to show the blood line. Toss watercress in the bowl with oil and caper juice and scatter over salmon. Sprinkle with capers and season with cracked black pepper.

Tip: This is yummy served with fresh bagels or sour dough.

Swiss Salad

SERVES 4

- *1 celeriac, peeled and coarsely grated*
- *2 red apples, sliced*
- *3 tbs. mayonnaise*
- *1 tbs. mustard*

Pop celeriac and apples in a bowl, coat with dressing.

Optional: Serve with a splash of lemon juice if you have it as it stops discolouration.

Tip: Celeriac combines the flavours of celery and parsley with a hint of nuttiness. Choose one which is pale, of medium size, with a slight greenish colouring on the top and no visible wrinkling. Cooking with celeriac is still quite underutilised, but beyond the unglamorous exterior and the challenge of peeling it, it has an extraordinary flavour, almost non-existent calories and a rich nutritious texture.

Sunny Salad

SERVES 6

- *2 ripe pineapples, cut into bite size chunks*
- *1 cup sultanas*
- *½ cup (125ml) sweet chilli ginger sauce*
- *1 cup shredded coconut, toasted*

Combine ingredients in a bowl and mix well. Season and serve.

Tip: Toasted coconut still has the same basic flavour as raw, but it also has a caramelised nuttiness and a crisp-chewy texture that raw doesn't.

Sweet Summer Salad

SERVES 2

Recipe from Heather Coombes.

- *1 mango, chopped*
- *1 small red onion, sliced into rings*
- *2 cups freshly diced pineapple*
- *8 cherry tomatoes, halved*

Place all ingredients into a serving bowl and mix ... Presto you're ready to serve!

Watermelon & Pistachio Dukkah

SERVES 8

- ¼ cup coriander seeds
- 2 tbs. cumin seeds
- 1 cup pistachio kernels
- 2.5 kg piece seedless watermelon, peeled, chilled

Cook coriander seeds, cumin seeds and pistachios with a smattering of sea salt and pepper in a non-stick frying pan over medium heat, stirring for 4 minutes or until aromatic. Set aside to cool. Place into a food processor and process until a coarse powder forms. Transfer to a bowl. Cut watermelon into cubes. Dip the top of each cube into the 'dukkah' and arrange on a serving plate. Serve with remaining dukkah.

Watermelon & Fetta Salad

SERVES 4

A recipe by the lovely Marcia Hines.

- 2 organic tomatoes
- ¼ of a watermelon
- 100g of fetta
- 12 mint leaves, chopped

Marcia explains: "I first tried this salad on tour in Tasmania, it is not only delicious but it looks beautiful too. Slice tomatoes then cut the watermelon into pieces roughly the same size. Dice the fetta into small pieces and sprinkle the mint leaves on top. Mix together and enjoy! "

Potato & Rice

I am both a student and a teacher in all my relationships.

Deepak Chopra

There are over 500 potato varieties available for gardeners to grow. Knowing which ones are best suited for what purpose can mean the difference between a delightfully smooth, creamy mash and a lumpy one or crispy, golden roasted potatoes or not!

As a general guide here is a little table we hope helps you in your quest for the 'perfect tater!'

POTATOES	VARIETIES
High starch content potatoes are the best mashers	Yukon Gold, Russet, King Edwards and Desiree
High water content potatoes are better for frying or in potato salads	Red skinned potatoes, Pink Fir, Kipfler, Charlotte, Patrone and Pink Eyes
Baking & Roasting Potatoes	Clean washed yellow skinned potatoes from any supermarket, Desiree, Nadine, Colban and Serbago

Avocado Mash

SERVES 4

Recipe inspired by the beautiful Janine Langer.

- *2 medium avocados*
- *700g Yukon gold potatoes*
- *½ cup (125ml) milk*
- *1 tsp. lemon juice*

Peel, quarter and wash the potatoes. Place the potatoes into a large pot with enough cold, salted water to cover them. Bring to boil and simmer for 15–20 minutes or until soft. Meanwhile, in a bowl, mash the avocados add lemon juice and stir until smooth. Gently warm the milk in the microwave. When potatoes are tender, drain and mash slowly adding the milk till smooth, then lightly fold in avocado mixture. Serve warm.

Tip: For a nice creamy mash, always add liquid/cream whilst potatoes are really hot.

Hint: Using a small crockpot is a great way to keep potatoes creamy and warm while waiting to serve.

Celeriac Potato Purée

SERVES 4

- *2 bulbs celeriac, peeled and sliced*
- *400g potato, peeled and sliced*
- *2 cups (500ml) chicken stock*
- *4 tbs. freshly chopped parsley*

Place all ingredients (except parsley) in a medium pot. Bring to boil and simmer for 15–20 minutes or until soft. Drain, season with cracked black pepper and parsley then puree.

Chat Potatoes with Rosemary & Garlic

SERVES 8

Inspired by Deb Moore.

- *2kg chat potatoes*
- *2 cloves garlic, sliced*
- *1 sprig of rosemary*
- *4 tbs. (60ml) olive oil*

Preheat oven 200°C. Halve the chat potatoes and using a small knife, cut a split into the rounded top of each potato. Insert a slice of garlic and a small sprig of rosemary into each potato. Pop potatoes into a roasting pan, drizzle with olive oil and season with sea salt and pepper. Bake for 40 minutes or until crisp and golden.

Cumin & Sweet Potato Mash

SERVES 4

- *500g sweet potato (kumara), peeled*
- *1 tbs. cumin seeds, toasted*
- *3 tbs. (45g) butter*
- *3 tbs. liquid chicken stock*

In a medium pot boil sweet potato till soft. Drain, return to low heat, add remaining ingredients, season and mash.

Tip: Cumin is the second most popular spice in the world, black pepper is number one. Cumin is a key component in both chilli powder and curry powder.

Double Baked Chive Potatoes

SERVES 4

- 4 potatoes, washed
- ½ cup sour cream
- 2–3 tbs. Gourmet Garden Chives

Preheat oven 200°C. With a sharp knife, pierce each potato 2-3 times before wrapping in alfoil. Place on a baking tray and bake for 1 hour (or until tender when pierced with a fork). Remove and allow to cool, make deep cuts in the top of each potato and remove the cooked flesh, leaving the skin intact. Mash the potato with créme fraiche and chives. Pile the mixture back into the potato skins. Return the potatoes to the oven and bake for a further 10 minutes.

Optional: As a general rule, a typical 300g potato should be baked for approx.1 hour.

Fragrant Rice

SERVES 4

- 1 cup (185g) long-grain rice, rinsed
- 1 star-anise
- 1 cinnamon stick
- 1 pinch saffron

Bring water to a boil in a saucepan over high heat. Stir in rice and spices and immediately reduce heat to low. Cover pan and simmer for 20 minutes or until rice is tender and liquid is absorbed. Remove from heat and let it stand for 5 minutes, covered. Fluff with a fork, discard the spices and serve.

Golden Baked Chips

SERVES 4

- *4 extra large potatoes, washed but leave skin on*
- *2 tbs. (30ml) olive oil*

Preheat oven 220°C. Cut potatoes into chunky chips about 1½ cm thick. Pat dry and place into a large bowl with olive oil and seasoning of your choice. Place chips in a thick based baking dish and bake for 25 minutes or until golden brown. Turn occasionally.

Optional: Nice served with sour cream and sweet chilli sauce to dip.

Orange Scented Jasmine Rice

SERVES 6

- *2 oranges, peeled*
- *2 cups (370g) jasmine rice, rinsed*

Pour 4 cups of water into a saucepan with orange peel and bring to the boil. Add rice and stirring bring to the boil. Cover and reduce heat to a simmer. Cook for 20 minutes or until tender. Fluff with fork before serving.

Pea & Potato Mash

SERVES 6

- 700g potatoes, peeled and cubed
- 140g peas
- 50g crème fraiche (or sour cream)
- 25g parmesan cheese

Boil potatoes for 10 minutes. Add peas, cook for 4 minutes then drain. Mash together before adding crème fraiche and parmesan, season and serve.

Potato & Cheese Puffs

MAKES 16

- 2–3 cups cold mashed potato
- 2 free range eggs, separated
- ½ cup grated cheese

Preheat oven 180°C. Combine potato with egg yolks, cheese, salt and pepper and mix together. Beat egg whites until stiff and fold into potato mixture. Using a dessert spoon, drop mixture onto a paper lined baking tray. Bake for 15–20 minutes or until set and golden brown.

Sesame Rice

SERVES 4

- 1½ cups (280g) long grain rice, rinsed
- 1 tbs. sesame oil
- 2 tbs. sesame seeds, toasted
- 2 spring onions, finely chopped

Bring 2½ cups water to the boil in a medium saucepan. Stir in rice and bring to boil before lowering heat, cover with a lid. Cook for 15 minutes or until water is absorbed and rice is tender. Remove from heat and allow to stand, covered, for 5 minutes. Using a fork, fluff to separate grains. Stir in remaining three ingredients.

Mustard Mashed Potatoes

SERVES 4

- 4 potatoes, peeled, quartered
- 4 tbs. (60g) softened butter
- ½ cup (125ml) milk (maybe more)
- 3 tbs. wholegrain mustard

Cook potatoes in a large pot of boiling, salted water for 20–25 minutes or until tender. Drain. Add butter and mash potatoes until almost smooth. Mix in milk and mustard and mash. Season to taste with sea salt and pepper.

Smashed Herbed Potato

SERVES 4–6

- 500g potatoes, cut into chunks
- 5 tbs. (75g) softened butter
- 6 chives, chopped
- 1 tbs. freshly chopped rosemary

In a saucepan add a tsp. of salt and potatoes, cover with water and bring to the boil. Reduce heat and cook for 15–20 minutes. Once soft, drain and smash with a fork. Add butter and herbs, mix and season.

Truffled Mashed Potatoes

SERVES 6–8

- 1kg white russet potatoes, peeled, cut into chunks
- ½ cup (125ml) cream
- 2 tbs. (30g) butter, softened
- 1 tbs. (15ml) white truffle oil

Simmer potatoes in a large saucepan of salted, boiling water for 15–20 minutes or until tender when pierced with a fork. Drain and return to pot. Mash potatoes with a potato masher (or potato ricer for a velvety, smooth finish) until there are no lumps. Add cream gradually and continue to stir. Add butter and truffle oil. Season to taste with sea salt and pepper.

Wasabi Mashed Potatoes

SERVES 4

- *1 medium head of garlic*
- *8 potatoes*
- *½ cup (125ml) milk*
- *4 tsp. wasabi powder*

Preheat oven 200°C. Remove papery outer skin of garlic. Place onto a baking paper lined tray and bake for 30–40 minutes (or until skin can be easily pierced with a fork). While garlic is roasting, peel and quarter the potatoes. Place in a large saucepan and cover with water. Bring to the boil, reduce heat and simmer for 15 minutes or until soft. Drain, and mash with milk until smooth and fluffy. Squeeze softened garlic cloves into potatoes. In a separate bowl, mix wasabi powder with just enough water to form a thick paste. Add to potatoes and mash altogether, add more milk if required and mash until light and fluffy. Season with sea salt and pepper and serve hot.

Tip: Wasabi is sometimes referred to as Japanese Horseradish and like horseradish, it is a root that is grated or sliced for use in cooking. For those who cannot find the genuine root, wasabi pastes and powders are available in nearly all supermarkets these days and will work nearly as well as the root.

Vegetables

Foods without labels are the healthiest foods you can get

Green Grocers Worldwide!

Beans with Lemon & Sesame

SERVES 4

- *1 tbs. (15ml) sesame oil*
- *80g fresh green beans, top 'n' tailed*
- *½ lemon*
- *1 tbs. sesame seeds*

Heat oil in a frying pan, add beans and fry for 2 minutes. Drizzle with lemon juice and add sesame seeds. Cook for another 2 minutes or until beans are done.

Optional: These are lovely served with fish cakes, chicken patties or casseroles and stews.

Tip: Eating at least 5 vegetables every day is critical to promoting good health. In this section we aim to inspire different ways to prepare vegetables to make them more interesting and more enjoyable for the entire family.

Braised Witlof

SERVES 4–6

- *2 tbs. (30g) butter*
- *4 whole witlof, washed*
- *1 cup (250ml) chicken or vegetable stock*

Preheat oven 180°C. Place witlof in a baking dish, brush with melted butter and season with sea salt and pepper. Pour over stock until dish is half full. Cover witlof closely with baking paper then cover dish with lid or foil. Bake for 20 minutes. Remove dish from oven and turn witlof, return to oven uncovered and bake for a further 20 minutes until witlof is tender and the sauce has reduced and is sticky.

Optional: Scatter with a layer of breadcrumbs after the first 20 minutes or add some grated gruyere cheese.

Spinach with Fetta

SERVES 4

- *200g spinach*
- *1 tbs. (15g) butter*
- *1 tsp. grated nutmeg*
- *100g fetta, crumbled*

Wilt spinach in butter in a large saucepan over a medium heat for a few minutes. Once wilted, sprinkle with nutmeg, stir in fetta and serve straight away.

Tip: When researching the health benefits of spinach there were so many we could write a book just on them! Know that spinach is a nutritional powerhouse and the more ways you can learn to prepare it for your family's consumption the better ... Good Luck!

Kale with Lemon & Paprika

SERVES 4

- 1 kale cabbage
- ⅛ tsp. paprika
- ½ lemon, juiced
- 1 tsp. olive oil

Add a small amount of water to the bottom of the saucepan. Strip kale of the central vein, chop into small pieces, and add to the water. Bring to the boil, add remaining ingredients and cover. Lower heat and simmer until kale turns a dull, green colour. Drizzle with olive oil prior to serving and toss.

Optional: Can substitute kale for spinach, baby spinach or silverbeet.

Carrot & Celeriac Mash

SERVES 4

- 350g celeriac, peeled and sliced
- 500g carrots, peeled and sliced
- 2 tbs. (30g) butter
- 1 tbs. flat leaf parsley, finely chopped

Place celeriac and carrots into a large saucepan and cover with boiling water. Add a little salt, pop on a lid and boil for 15 minutes or until tender. Drain and return to the pan. Add butter and mash. Season and serve, sprinkled with parsley.

Optional: Serve with a knob of butter.

Tip: Choose celeriac which is pale, with a slight greenish colouring on the top and no visible wrinkling. Celeriac provides us with potassium, calcium and vitamin C, and contains just 14 calories per 100g. It has a wonderful ability to absorb flavours, and is very tasty. The whole bulb can be eaten, and the leaves are excellent for flavouring soups.

Caramelised Chicory

SERVES 4

- *1 tbs. (15g) butter*
- *4 heads chicory, trimmed and halved lengthways*
- *2 tsp. honey*
- *½ large orange, juice only*

Preheat oven 180°C. Spread half the butter thickly over the bottom of an ovenproof dish, then arrange the chicory halves in a single layer in a dish. Drizzle with honey and orange juice, season with sea salt and pepper. Roast uncovered, for an hour, turning and basting the chicory every 15 minutes. Take the dish out of the oven when the juices have reduced to a few spoonfuls of thick syrup and the chicory is caramelised. Serve warm.

Chunky Wedges

SERVES 4

- *200g carrots, peeled and cut into wedges*
- *200g swede, peeled and cut into wedges*
- *1 tbs. (15ml) olive oil*
- *½ tsp. ground coriander*

Preheat oven to 180°C. Place carrot and swede in a saucepan. Cover with cold water. Bring to the boil, then cook, partially covered, for 10 minutes or until almost tender. Drain. Combine vegetable wedges, with oil and coriander in a baking dish. Toss to coat. Bake for 15 minutes or until golden.

Optional: This is really nice made with potatoes and sweet potato (kumara) too.

Tip: Serve with a spiced sour cream by mixing a little sour cream, yoghurt, chilli flakes and lemon zest together.

Corn Purée

SERVES 4

- 1 cup (250ml) chicken stock
- 4 corn cobs
- 1 onion, finely diced
- 3 tbs. chopped coriander

In a pot bring stock to simmer, add corn and onion and return to boil. Reduce heat and simmer for 8 minutes or until corn is nice and soft. Remove from heat, drain and allow to cool. Slice kernels from the cobs and place into a food processor with onions, puree. Scrape out into a serving dish, fold through coriander, season with pepper and serve.

Optional: This is also fabulous un-pureed. It's flavoursome, textured and a great accompaniment to nearly any main meal ... D.e.l.i.c.i.o.u.s!

Gingered Brussels Sprouts

SERVES 4

- 500g Brussels sprouts
- 2 tbs. (30ml) lemon juice
- 1 tsp. fresh ginger
- 1 tsp. lemon zest

Cut a cross into the base of each sprout. Steam for 8 minutes then drain water, cover and allow to dry. Sprinkle lemon juice and ginger over the sprouts, toss well and add lemon rind. Cover pan and leave to stand for 5 minutes before serving.

Ginger & Broccoli Sautéed Salad

SERVES 2

- 1 tbs. chopped ginger
- 200g broccoli, cut into similar sized florets
- 1 small red onion, diced
- 1–2 tbs. soya sauce

Into a wok or non-stick frying pan, add ¼ cup water and ginger. Cook briefly then add the broccoli and onion. Stir-fry for 3–4 minutes, until almost tender. Add the soya sauce and serve with grilled chicken, fish or tofu.

Optional: This is particularly nice served with Seared Thai Salmon (see Fish & Seafood).

Green Beans Almondine

SERVES 4

A great side dish for roast duck.

- 100g French green beans
- 1 tbs. (15g) butter
- ⅔ cup sliced almonds (crushed under a rolling pin)

Snap the ends off both sides of the beans. In a large, non-stick frying pan add 1½ cups of water and bring to a boil. Add beans and quickly steam (turning beans frequently) for approximately 4–5 minutes, then drain. In the same pan melt butter and add beans. Cover and reduce heat to a simmer. Cook on a low heat for approximately 6–7 minutes. Drain off excess butter. Add crushed almonds and gently toss. Lightly salt before serving.

Grilled Zucchinis with Mustard

SERVES 6

- 500g zucchinis, cut in half lengthways
- 2 tbs. (30g) butter, melted
- 1 tbs. wholegrain mustard

Brush zucchinis with melted butter and place them cut side down on a BBQ or pre-heated grill. Grill until brown. Turn once and spread with the mustard. Continue to grill until golden.

Italian Herbs with BBQ Corn

SERVES 4

- 4 corn cobs
- 4 tsp. butter
- 4 tsp. Gourmet Garden Italian Herbs

Remove husk from corn cobs. Place each on a large piece of foil. Top with a knob of butter and a squeeze of Gourmet Garden Italian Herbs. Seal parcel tightly. Cook on BBQ for 10–15 minutes, turning regularly. *Enjoy!*

Maple Syrup Parsnips

SERVES 4

- 1kg parsnips, peeled, quartered lengthways
- ¼ cup (62ml) olive oil
- 3 tbs. pure maple syrup

Preheat the oven to 180°C. Place the parsnips into a roasting tin. Pour the oil over the parsnips and mix them well so that the oil completely coats all pieces. Pour the maple syrup over the parsnips and transfer the roasting tin to the oven. Roast the parsnips for 35 minutes, or until they are tender and golden brown.

Minty Peas

SERVES 4

- 2 cups fresh peas
- 1 tbs. Gourmet Garden mint
- 1 tbs. (15ml) freshly squeezed lemon juice

Boil peas and instead of coating them in butter, toss through mint and lemon juice. *Herbal and healthy!*

Paprika Buttered Corn

MAKES 4

- 4 cobs of corn
- 2 tbs. (30g) butter
- 1 tsp. paprika
- 1 lemon

Into a large pot of boiling water add corn cobs and boil for 6–8 minutes. Meanwhile, in a cup mash together butter, paprika and the zest of the lemon. Remove corn from heat, drain and bathe with the savoury butter.

Pesto Broccoli

SERVES 4

- 300g broccoli
- 1 tbs. freshly chopped mint
- 2 tbs. basil pesto
- 2 tbs. pine nuts, toasted

Steam broccoli florets for 5–6 minutes or until tender. Meanwhile, stir the mint leaves into the pesto. Place the broccoli on a serving dish, coat in pesto and sprinkle with pine nuts.

Tip: Broccoli contains twice the vitamin C of an orange. It has almost as much calcium as whole milk and it has incredible antioxidant properties.

Roast Beetroot

SERVES 4–6

- 6 beetroots, peeled and quartered
- 3 tbs. (45ml) olive oil
- 2 twigs fresh rosemary

Preheat oven 200°C. Toss beetroot in olive oil, season with sea salt and pepper and sprinkle with fresh rosemary leaves. Bake for 30–40 minutes or until tender.

Tip: For optimal flavour, bake beets instead of boiling or steaming with their skin on to retain nutrients. Wrap them in foil first.

Roasted Beetroot & Orange

SERVES 6

- 8 baby beetroots
- 2 oranges, peeled and segmented, reserving the juice
- 3 tbs. (45ml) olive oil
- 1 tsp. French mustard

Trim the leaves off the top of the beetroot, rinse the beets in cold water, place in a large saucepan and cover with cold water. Bring to the boil, turn down to simmer and cook until tender, approx. 30–40 minutes. When cooked, cool under cold running water while removing the skins (use your hands) and leave to drain. Cut the beetroots into quarters and place in an oven dish. Coat with ½ the oil. Place in a 200°C oven for 15 –20 minutes. Cool and serve with orange segments and drizzled with a salad dressing made by whisking together juice, oil and mustard. Serve seasoned with sea salt and pepper. .

Tip: Don't throw away the healthy leafy greens, prepare them as you would cabbage, kale, or spinach. When very fresh, beetroot leaves are tender and sweet and taste almost like spinach. As they age, they become tougher and develop a much stronger and unsavoury flavor.

Roasted Butternut Squash

SERVES 6–8

- 500g butternut squash (pumpkin)
- 2 tbs. (30ml) macadamia nut oil
- 2 tbs. honey
- 2 tbs. fresh thyme leaves

Preheat oven 180°C. Peel butternut, remove seeds and cut into chunks roughly the same size. Place in a baking tray that has been coated with oil. Drizzle with honey and thyme, roast for 30–40 minutes or until turning gold and tender.

Roasted Garlic

SERVES 4

- 4 fresh garlic bulbs
- ¼ cup (62ml) olive oil

Preheat oven 180°C. Peel away the outer layers of the garlic bulb leaving the skin of the individual cloves intact. Using a knife cut ½ cm off the top of cloves exposing the flesh of each. Place garlic heads in a baking pan and drizzle a couple of teaspoons of oil over each head, cover with alfoil. Bake for 30 minutes or until the cloves feel soft when pressed. Allow to cool so you can touch it without burning yourself.

Hint: Eat as is or mash with a fork and use for cooking. Can be spread over warm French bread, mixed with sour cream for a topping for baked potatoes or mixed in with parmesan and pasta ... Soooo flavoursome and so many health benefits!

Roasted Swede

SERVES 4

- *400g swede, peeled and cut into chunky fingers*
- *2 tbs. (30ml) olive oil*
- *2 twigs fresh rosemary, leaves removed*
- *12 sage leaves*

Preheat oven 180°C. Toss swede in olive oil and roast with rosemary and sage for 20 minutes or until tender and golden. Serve seasoned with sea salt.

Roasted Tomatoes

SERVES 4–6

- *1kg vine-ripened cherry tomatoes*
- *2 tbs. (30ml) olive oil*
- *2 tbs. (30ml) balsamic vinegar*

Preheat oven 220°C. Line a baking tray with baking paper, pop tomatoes on the tray and drizzle with oil and vinegar. Season with ground pepper and roast for about 15 minutes or until tomatoes just start to collapse.

Tip: Tomatoes are the world's most popular fruit.

Sautéed Cabbage

SERVES 4

- 2 tbs. (30g) ghee
- 2 baby fennel bulbs, trimmed and thinly sliced
- ½ small, green cabbage, shredded
- 2 tbs. fresh thyme leaves

Heat ghee in a non-stick frying pan over medium-high heat. Cook fennel for 1–2 minutes. Add cabbage and cook for a further 2–3 minutes or until the mixture softens slightly. Remove from heat and stir through thyme leaves. Season with sea salt and pepper.

Sautéed Mushrooms

SERVES 4

- 300g button mushrooms, halved
- 1 clove garlic, crushed
- 2 tbs. (30g) butter
- ½ tsp. dried oregano

Sauté mushrooms and garlic in butter for 6-8 minutes or until mushrooms are tender. Stir in oregano and season with sea salt and pepper.

Optional: To keep mushrooms white and firm when sautéeing, add a splash of lemon juice to the butter.

Tip: Mushrooms grow from spores not seeds. A single mature mushroom will drop as many as 16 billion spores. There are over 38,000 varieties of mushrooms, some edible, some very poisonous.

Spinach & Apricot

SERVES 4

A great way to serve spinach!

- 6 dried apricots, chopped
- 1 tsp. butter
- 2 spring onions, ends trimmed, thinly sliced
- 100g baby spinach leaves (or silverbeet)

Place the apricots in a small heatproof bowl and cover with boiling water. Set aside for 10 minutes to soak. Drain. Meanwhile, melt the butter in a non-stick frying pan over medium heat. Add the onions stirring for 1 minute or until soft. Add the spinach, stirring for 2 minutes or until the spinach wilts. Add the apricots to the mixture and stir to combine. Season with sea salt and pepper.

Spinach with Pine Nuts

SERVES 4–6

- 1–2 tbs. ghee
- 1 bunch fresh spinach, chopped
- ¼ cup pine nuts, toasted

Over medium heat, melt ghee in a saucepan with a glass lid. Add 2 tbs. water and spinach, cover, stir and cook for 10 minutes. Season with a light sprinkle of sea salt and stir through pine nuts.

Optional: Can substitute spinach for cabbage especially the richly flavoured curly kale.

Stuffed Zucchini

SERVES 4

- *2 medium zucchinis*
- *2 tbs. (30ml) garlic infused olive oil*
- *½ red onion, finely chopped*
- *2 cups soft bread cubes*

Wash zucchini and cook whole in a small amount of boiling water for about 6–7 minutes. Drain and cut into halves lengthwise. Scoop out pulp and chop. Melt oil in a small non-stick frying pan, sauté onion until tender, stir in chopped pulp, bread cubes and season with sea salt and pepper. Stuff zucchini with bread mixture. Place in a greased baking dish and bake at 180°C for 20 minutes or until tender.

Optional: Sprinkle with some parmesan cheese before baking.

Sweet Potato Rosti

SERVES 4

- *550g orange sweet potato (kumara), peeled*
- *4 tbs. (60ml) olive oil*
- *1 clove garlic, crushed*
- *½ cup freshly grated parmesan cheese*

Using a vegetable peeler, slice the sweet potato into thin ribbon-like strips. Toss the sweet potato in the oil, add garlic and parmesan and season to taste. Place in rounds in a heated frying pan and cook for 2 minutes before turning. Cook a further 1–2 minutes, remove and serve.

Optional: This is delicious served with the Egg White & Mushroom Omelette (see: Breakfasts).

Sweet & Sour Cabbage Wedges

SERVES 4

- *2 tbs. (30ml) olive oil*
- *½ head baby cabbage or sugar loaf, quartered through the core*
- *½ cup (125ml) cider vinegar*
- *2 tbs. sugar*

Heat olive oil in a frypan over medium heat. Cook cabbage for 3 minutes each side or until golden brown. Add vinegar, sugar and 1½ cups water, reduce heat and simmer for 15 minutes.

Zucchinis with Lemon & Mint

SERVES 4

- *4 medium zucchini, halved lengthways, roughly chopped*
- *1 lemon, juice and zest*
- *1 tbs. (15ml) olive oil*
- *2 tbs. small fresh mint leaves*

Preheat oven 200°C. Place zucchini, juice, zest and oil in a baking dish. Season with sea salt and pepper. Toss to combine. Roast for 15–20 minutes or until zucchini is tender. Top with mint leaves. Serve.

Optional: Serve with grilled fish or chicken breast.

Mains

Our bodies have an inner intelligence. In other words, they know exactly what it is we need to eat (and when) for us to be healthy.

Deepak Chopra

Poultry

Baked Chicken with Honey & Cumin

SERVES 2

- *¼ cup honey*
- *2 garlic cloves, crushed*
- *1 tsp. ground cumin*
- *6 free range chicken drumsticks*

Mix the first three ingredients. Make diagonal slits into the drumsticks and coat with glaze. Cover, refrigerate and marinate for at least 2 hours. Place in a shallow baking dish, use all marinade to ensure chicken is coated. Cook in a 180°C oven for 40 minutes (cover lightly with foil if browning too much) or until chicken is done. Turn once during cooking.

Optional: Delicious sliced over a fresh, green salad.

Hint: It typically takes 2–4 hours for a marinade to flavour chicken nicely. Removing the skin helps absorbs marinades. As does slicing the meat. For a strong, tangy marinade, use vinegar or lemon juice. For something spicy, add pepper. Other seasonings that complement chicken are yoghurt, salt and mustard. Fresh herbs also offer a beautiful flavour. If the herbs are dry, crush before using to release their scents quickly.

Balsamic Chicken

SERVES 4

Recipe from Dymphna Boholt.

- *4 tbs. (60ml) balsamic vinegar*
- *2 tbs. brown sugar*
- *1 clove garlic, crushed*
- *4 free range chicken thighs*

Combine vinegar, sugar and garlic and pour over chicken thighs. Marinate for 1–2 hours. Grill or roast in a 180°C oven for 40 minutes or until cooked through and sauce has caramelised.

Optional: Serve with steamed greens.

BBQ Chilli Chicken

SERVES 4

- *14 free range chicken tenderloins*
- *2 tbs. sambel oelek*
- *2 limes, juiced*
- *1 cup (250ml) tamari soy sauce*

In a large bowl mix all ingredients and season. Allow to marinate for at least 2 hours. Thread chicken onto a bamboo skewer and cook on a medium grill or BBQ.

Cajun Chicken Pineapple Skewers

MAKES 10

- *2 tbs. (30ml) macadamia nut oil*
- *2 tbs. Cajun spice*
- *400g diced free range chicken*
- *1 pineapple, diced*

Mix the oil in a bowl with Cajun spice and chicken. On a wet bamboo skewer, place a piece of chicken then pineapple until all mix is used. Cook skewers on the BBQ.

Tip: Soak skewers in water to avoid splintering when applied to heat.

Hint: Cajun cuisine originated with the French Arcadian people after they immigrated from Canada into Louisiana in the US. Like many spice blends, the composition of Cajun spice mixes vary, but commonly used ingredients include: Paprika, cayenne pepper, garlic powder, black pepper, oregano and onion powder.

Chicken, Apple & Cherry Stuffing

SERVES 4

- *4 free range chicken breasts*
- *100g dried apples*
- *1 cup cherries, halved and de-stoned*
- *1 cup walnuts, chopped*

Preheat oven 180°C. Butterfly each breast and season. Take a 40cm piece of greaseproof paper and a 40cm piece of foil. Place greaseproof on top of foil. Place chicken lengthways. Combine rest of ingredients to form the stuffing. Place stuffing in the middle of the chicken and roll tightly, twisting both ends to form what should look like a bonbon! Cook for 35 minutes.

Optional: Serve sliced accompanied by Red Onion Marmalade (see: Sauces, Salsas & Marinades).

Chicken Curry

MAKES 4

Very easy and very yummy!

- *1 roasted chicken, remove skin*
- *225g natural yoghurt*
- *6 tbs. mayonnaise*
- *2 tbs. curry powder*

Preheat oven 175°C. Chop the roast chicken into bite size pieces. In a bowl mix together yoghurt, mayo and curry powder. Marinate chicken pieces in yoghurt mixture for at least 1 hour then bake in a moderate oven for 15–20 minutes or until heated through.

Optional: Serve with rice, fresh coriander and lemon wedges.

Tip: Curry powder is a blend of spices and varies on the region it stems from. India tend to use garam masala the way the west uses curry powder. Curry powder is based largely on four spices: Coriander, cumin, fenugreek and turmeric, with the possibility of many other ingredients being included.

Chicken Scallop Curry

SERVES 2

Recipe by the lovely Dan Primmer.

- *400g can coconut cream*
- *2 tbs. Thai red curry paste*
- *300g free range chicken, diced*
- *20 scallops*

Place coconut cream in a non-stick frying pan and heat to a simmer. Add paste and stir until mixed. Add chicken and simmer for 10 minutes. Add scallops, cook for 2 minutes each side, remove from heat and serve over rice.

Optional: Add thinly sliced red capsicums when adding scallops.

Chicken & Vegie Patties

MAKES 12

- *450g lean free range chicken mince*
- *½ cup organic mango & apple cereal*
- *¼ cup finely grated zucchini*
- *¼ cup finely grated carrot*

Combine all ingredients in a large bowl and mix well. Shape mixture into patties. Heat a frying pan over medium heat. Cook patties for 3–4 minutes each side or until cooked through.

Optional: These are absolutely sensational served with Mango Mayonnaise (see: Sauces, Salsas & Marinades).

Chicken with Warm Tomato Salsa

SERVES 2

- *2 free range chicken thighs*
- *1 large ox-heart tomato*
- *1 spring onion, thinly sliced*
- *2 tbs. (30ml) caramelised balsamic vinegar*

Heat a non-stick fry pan, add a tbs. of water and cook chicken for 5 minutes on each side. Remove from pan and sit, covered. Chop tomato into cubes retaining their juice. Combine tomato, onion, balsamic vinegar and 2 tbs. water with sea salt and pepper in the frying pan. Add chicken back, reduce heat and simmer for 4 minutes or until chicken is tender on the inside. Slice to serve and top with the tangy salsa from the pan.

Cranberry & Orange Turkey

SERVES 6

- *4 kg turkey*
- *4 large oranges, cut in half*
- *2 tbs. orange marmalade*
- *¼ cup (62ml) cranberry sauce*

Preheat oven 180°C. Place orange wedges in both body and neck cavities of turkey, fold neck skin, fasten with skewers and season with sea salt and pepper. Place turkey, breast side up, on a rack in a large shallow roasting pan, roast for 3–4 hours. Combine marmalade and sauce and microwave for 30 seconds or until melted. Brush the glaze over the turkey during the last 20 minutes of roasting time. Remove turkey from the oven and allow to rest for 10 minutes before carving. Place on a large, warm platter and garnish.

Creamy Tomato & Basil Chicken

SERVES 4

- 500g cherry tomatoes, halved
- 4 free range chicken breasts, sliced
- 250ml cooking cream
- ¼ cup basil, torn

In a non-stick frying pan, add 2 tbs. water and sauté cherry tomatoes for 2 minutes, set aside. Into same pan, sauté chicken for 4–5 minutes, turning once. Add the cream, season with sea salt and pepper and stir to melt over a low heat. Simmer for 4–5 minutes or until slightly thickened, add tomatoes and basil and mix. Serve warm.

Optional: Delicious served with soft polenta or parmesan mash, which is easily made by boiling potatoes and adding warm milk and butter, mashing then stirring through finely grated parmesan cheese.

Fried Chicken with Goats Cheese

SERVES 4

- 4 chicken breast fillets
- 100g goats cheese
- 2 tbs. lemon thyme leaves
- 4 tbs. (60ml) olive oil

Preheat oven 180°C. Make a pocket in each chicken breast, keeping the opening narrow. Fill the pocket with the combined mix of goats cheese and lemon thyme leaves and seal with a toothpick. Sprinkle with seasoning. Heat the oil in a non-stick frying pan over medium/high heat. Add the chicken and cook for 2–3 minutes each side or until golden. Transfer to a paper lined baking tray and bake for 10 minutes or until cooked through.

Optional: If lemon thyme leaves are unavailable, use fresh thyme leaves.

Hoi Sin Duck Rolls

MAKES 8

- 400g roasted duck, shredded
- 1 cup (250ml) hoi sin sauce
- 1 pkt rice paper sheets
- 1 pkt snow pea sprouts

Place duck in a non-stick frying pan while gradually adding the sauce on gentle heat. Remove from heat. Soften rice paper sheets by soaking them individually in water. Place on a clean surface and dollop a tbs. of ingredients in the middle of the sheet, top with snow pea sprouts and roll and fold until it resembles a spring roll. Make sure you use a damp tea towel to stop rice paper rolls drying out. Serve with Dipping Sauce (see: Sauces, Salsas & Marinades).

Honey Chilli Chicken Drumsticks

SERVES 4

Recipe from Joan Gilbert Smith.

- 12 free range chicken drumsticks
- ½ cup (125ml) tamari soy sauce
- ¼ cup (85g) honey
- 2 tbs. (30ml) sweet chilli sauce

Preheat oven 180°C. Mix a paste from last three ingredients, coat drumsticks well and place in a non-stick baking dish, cook for about 45 minutes or until done.

Honey Glazed Chicken with Broccolini

SERVES 4

- 4 free range chicken breasts, chopped
- ½ cup (160g) honey
- 12 pieces broccolini
- ½ cup flaked almonds, toasted

In a bowl, marinate the chicken with honey and set aside for 1 hour. In a non-stick frying pan, sauté chicken over a medium/high heat for 4–5 minutes or until cooked. Steam broccolini until tender. Place broccolini on a plate and top with chicken. Drizzle with any remaining sauce. Garnish generously with almonds.

Tip: You want your chicken breast to be nice and firm on the outside, but juicy and full of flavour on the inside.

Italian Chicken Meatballs

SERVES 4

- 500g free range chicken mince
- 4 tbs. semi dried tomato pesto
- 4 tbs. diced olives
- 1 cup fresh breadcrumbs

Combine mince, pesto, and olives and season. On a plate place breadcrumbs and sprinkle with water, allow to soak for a minute before mixing into mince mixture. Roll into meatballs, pan fry in a non-stick frying pan.

Optional: These are sensational served with your favourite Napolitano sauce.

Lemon Chicken

SERVES 4

This is incredibly flavoursome!

- *4 free range chicken breasts*
- *4 lemons, juiced and zested*
- *1 cup corn flour*
- *1 ltr. sunflower oil*

Cut chicken into thin strips. Place in a bowl add lemon juice and zest. Cover and refrigerate for 2 hours. Add corn flour, the mix should resemble a batter, if too runny add a little more corn flour. Heat half the oil in a small pot, fry a few pieces at a time giving the oil enough time to regain heat (replace oil if needed). Place chicken on a tray with absorbent towel to remove any excess oil. Season with sea salt and pepper then serve.

Mustard Chicken

SERVES 4

- *6 tbs. corn flour*
- *4 free range chicken breasts, cut into strips*
- *2 tbs. wholegrain mustard*
- *1 cup (250ml) chicken stock*

Season flour with sea salt and pepper. Toss chicken in seasoned flour to coat. Heat a non-stick frying pan and fry on all sides until lightly browned. Stir in stock and mustard and bring to the boil. Simmer uncovered for 5 minutes or until the chicken is cooked and sauce has thickened.

Orange Duck

SERVES 6

- *2 oranges*
- *2 garlic cloves , sliced*
- *1 large whole duck*
- *6 tbs. brown sugar*

Preheat oven 180°C. Juice the oranges and set aside. Cut the left over orange into chunks and combine with garlic. Stuff the duck. Mix orange juice and sugar. Place duck on a baking rack in a tray with 1 cup (250ml) of water. Brush duck with some of the orange and brown sugar glaze. Place in oven for approx. 1 hour, basting with orange syrup every 10 minutes. The duck is cooked when juices run clear and when tested with a skewer. When cooked, cut and serve.

Oyster Mushroom & Chicken Rolls

MAKES 8

- *200g free range chicken mince*
- *1 cup oyster mushrooms, sliced*
- *1 cup (250ml) teriyaki sauce*
- *1 pkt rice paper sheets*

In a non-stick frying pan cook the mince for 3 minutes, stir in mushrooms and gradually add sauce. Cook over medium heat for 5–6 minutes. Allow to cool. Soften rice paper sheets by soaking them in water. Place on a clean flat surface, dollop 2 tbs. of mixture in the middle of the sheet. Fold in the bottoms and roll until it resembles a spring roll. Serve immediately with any dipping sauce.

Tip: If you prepare ahead of time, cover with a damp tea towel to stop rice paper rolls drying out. Add any finely shredded vegetables you think your family will eat.

Poached Chicken with Passionfruit Dressing

SERVES 4

- 4 free range chicken breasts
- 6 fresh passionfruit
- 6 tbs. (90ml) rice wine vinegar
- 1 tbs. fresh chopped mint

In a large non-stick frying pan fill with three quarters of water. Place on heat and bring to boil. Add salt then chicken. Simmer and cook for 15 minutes or until chicken has been cooked through. Cut passionfruit, remove the pulp and place into a bowl with the rest of the ingredients, mix and serve over sliced chicken.

Portuguese Style Charcoal Chicken

SERVES 6

- 1 large free range chicken
- 6 cloves garlic, crushed
- 2 lemons, juiced
- 2 tsp. smoked paprika

Trim the chicken of excess fat. Use sharp scissors to cut through the breast bone. Open chicken out, turn over and flatten by pressing down on the back bone. Make a small cut under each wing, to help chicken flatten further. Make several cuts with a sharp knife to allow the flavours of the marinade to permeate. Combine garlic, lemon juice and paprika and mix well. Brush the chicken on both sides with mixture and sprinkle with sea salt, cover and marinate in fridge for 45 minutes. Cook chicken on a hot charcoal BBQ, turning frequently and baste continuously with the remaining marinade for 30 minutes or until golden brown. Cut chicken into pieces.

Optional: Serve with Piri Piri sauce to dip.

Roasted Chicken with Preserved Lemons

SERVES 4

- 3 tbs. (45ml) olive oil
- 4 potatoes, peeled and cut into chunks
- 1–1½ preserved lemons, skin only
- 8 free range chicken pieces

Preheat oven 190°C. Drizzle olive oil into the bottom of a large roasting pan. Spread the chunks of potato over the base, tucking in pieces of well washed lemon peel. Pour ½ cup of cold water into the pan, arrange chicken pieces on top and baste with liquid, season. Roast for 40–50 minutes or until potatoes are tender and chicken is cooked through.

Tip: To preserve your own lemons (see: Sauces, Salsas & Marinades) it is very easy to do and they will keep in a refrigerator (in a sterilised and sealed jar) for six months.

Satay Chicken

SERVES 2

A sensational recipe from Spud Moore.

- 1 tsp. red curry paste
- 1 large free range chicken breast, diced
- 1 tbs. peanut butter
- ½ cup (125ml) cream

In a non-stick frying pan, fry off red curry paste and add diced chicken. Seal until half cooked, add peanut butter and stir through cream. Simmer for 4 minutes or until chicken is tender.

Optional: Serve atop rice or fettuccine. Toss through some vegetables if you have them in your fridge.

Spiced Turkey Patties

MAKES 10–12

- *500g minced turkey*
- *1 tsp. ground cumin*
- *1 tsp. ground coriander*
- *1 onion, grated*

Mix all ingredients in a bowl with sea salt and pepper. Shape into meatballs and cook in a non-stick frying pan for 4 minutes each side or until browned and cooked through.

Optional: Serve in a wrap with salad and drizzled with Minted Yoghurt or Tahini Sauce (see: Sauces, Salsas & Marinades).

Stuffed Chicken Breast

SERVES 4

- *4 free range chicken breasts*
- *150g gorgonzola cheese, cut into small pieces*
- *12 pieces semi-dried tomatoes, halved (reserve some oil)*
- *1 tbs. freshly chopped tarragon*

Using a long, thin knife (and keeping the opening narrow), cut a horizontal slit along the thin, long edge of a chicken breast careful not to cut through. Using a narrow knife, cut pockets into chicken breast, mix together cheese, tomatoes and tarragon, fill pockets with mixture and secure with toothpicks. Heat 2 tbs. of oil from semi-dried tomatoes and pan fry chicken until cooked through.

Optional: Sensational served with a rocket salad.

Stuffed, Poached Chicken Breasts

SERVES 4

A little effort required, but worth it for the taste!

- *1 large apple, peeled and coarsely grated*
- *½ cup (100g) pitted prunes, chopped*
- *2 skinless free range chicken breast*

Place each chicken breast between two pieces of cling film and pound into thin pieces. Mix together prunes and apple and season. Place a spoonful of stuffing along the shorter side of each chicken breast, then roll up. Take two large sheets of plastic wrap and roll each breast in several layers of wrap. Tightly twist the ends of the wrap and gently roll the chicken breast back and forth to form a sausage shape. Tie ends with string to seal securely. Place inside a steamer in a saucepan with hot water. Bring water to boil, reduce the heat to low, cover the pan and poach the chicken for 45 minutes or until a skewer inserted into the centre of each roll feels hot on the back of your hand. Cool in the plastic. Serve by unwrapping and cutting in 5cm discs.

Optional: Serve with Red Onion Marmalade (see: Sauces, Salsas & Marinades).

Tip: When enjoying this dish, just remember that chickens are the closest living relative of the Tyrannosaurus-rex ... Which makes the 'Alektorophobia' (fear of chickens) slightly more plausible!

Tandoori Spatchcock

MAKES 2

- 2 spatchcocks
- 4 tbs. (80g) tandoori paste
- 250g Greek yoghurt
- 4 tbs. fresh mint

Preheat oven 180°C. Coat spatchcocks completely with tandoori. Season with salt and pepper. Place on baking tray and cook in an oven for 50–60 minutes. Mix mint and yoghurt. Cut spatchcock into quarters and drizzle with minted yoghurt.

Turkey Cakes

MAKES 12

- 675g turkey mince
- 1 small red onion, grated
- 2 tbs. fresh thyme leaves
- 2 tbs. (30ml) garlic infused olive oil

Mix all ingredients together reserving 1 tbs. oil. Heat a non-stick frying pan, brush cakes with remaining oil and cook for 4 minutes. Turn, brush with more oil and cook for a further 4 minutes or until cooked through. Serve immediately.

Turkey Involtini

SERVES 4

A sensational dinner that combines rich flavours and wraps them in tender turkey.

- *4 turkey breast*
- *2 large chargrilled capsicums*
- *2 tbs. basil pesto*
- *250g bocconcini or mozzarella*

Slice each turkey breast into 4 thin strips (for chicken, slice each breast in two) and place between sheets of baking paper. Gently flatten with a meat mallet. Place a piece of turkey breast on a clean chopping board with the short edge facing you, spread with pesto, then lay capsicum to fit within the turkey. Break bocconcini into pieces and place in the centre, roll up and secure with toothpicks. In a non stick frying pan, gently heat the rolls for about 8 minutes, turning regularly or until golden. Cover with foil and leave to rest for 5 minutes.

Optional: Pan can be deglazed with stock to create a sensational sauce.

Turkey Schnitzel

SERVES 4

- 4 turkey breasts
- ⅓ cup parmesan, grated
- ⅔ cup freshly grated breadcrumbs
- 2 free range eggs

Flatten turkey breasts using a mallet, mix grated parmesan with breadcrumbs on a plate and season with sea salt and pepper. Beat eggs in a bowl, dip turkey into egg then cover with breadcrumbs, leave to set in the fridge for approximately 10 minutes. Shallow fry for 3–4 minutes on each side until golden. Serve with lemon wedges and salad for a tasty, healthy meal.

Optional: Add 1 tsp. finely chopped herbs (sage or thyme) to breadcrumbs.

Whole Roast Quail

SERVES 2

Whole quail is very quick and easy to prepare and cook.

- 2 cloves of garlic
- 2 sprigs of fresh thyme
- 2 whole quails
- 2 tsp. olive oil

Preheat oven 180°C. Place a clove of garlic and a sprig of thyme into the cavity of each quail. Rub a tsp. of oil over each and season with some salt and pepper. Roast for 15–20 minutes.

Fish & Seafood

By increasing your intake of fish to twice a week,
you can decrease the chance of heart disease by a whopping 36%

Everyone knows that fish is good for you, we hear it all the time. It's high in protein and relatively low in fat. It's also a source of many vitamins and minerals. Eating fish regularly—as often as two to three times a week—may even reduce your risk of heart disease. Why then is cooking it so intimidating for so many of us?

Assuming you have a lovely fresh fillet approximately 2 cm thick, here are a few easy tips on how to cook it successfully.

1. **Grill**: *Brush fish with melted butter and season or marinate. Place in single layer on a well greased baking tray. Grill for 4–5 minutes. Baste during cooking. Turn halfway through.*

2. **Bake**: *Preheat oven to 180°C. Place fish in a greased baking dish. Brush with melted butter and season with sea salt and pepper. Flavour with basting sauce, lemon juice or fresh herbs and bake for 10 minutes.*

3. **Pan Fry**: *Heat olive oil or butter in a non-stick frying pan over medium/high heat. Coat fish with seasoned flour, dip in milk or beaten egg. Coat in seasoning again and cook 4–5 minutes per side or until done.*

4. **Poach**: *Fish responds well to being cooked in liquid kept just below boiling point. You can poach fish using water, wine, stock or milk. Bring liquid to a simmer, gently slip in fillets and cook for 8–10 minutes, adjusting the heat so that the liquid just trembles.*

5. **Steam**: *Is particularly good for rolled fillets of plaice, sole or trout, as they retain their shape perfectly and remain moist. Add 5 cm of boiling water to a saucepan, then fit the steamer over, making sure it doesn't come into contact with the water, cover and steam for 8–10 minutes or 7–8 minutes for rolled fillets.*

Tip: Fish is done when the colour turns from translucent to opaque (white).

Asian Salmon

SERVES 4

- *4 x 120g skinless salmon fillets*
- *½ cup (125ml) soy sauce*
- *2cm piece of ginger, finely shredded*
- *⅓ cup (85ml) sweet chilli sauce*

Preheat oven 180°C. Place fish in a shallow baking dish. Combine soy, ginger and sweet chilli and pour over fish. Cover with foil and bake for 8 minutes, or until just cooked through.

Baked Ginger Fish

SERVES 2

- *1 whole fish*
- *2 large chillis, remove seeds and membrane*
- *1 tbs. freshly grated ginger*
- *1 cup (250ml) mirin (sushi seasoning)*

Place 50cm of foil on a bench and cover with 50cm of greaseproof paper. Score the fish on both sides and rub chilli and ginger into each side. Let marinate for 30 minutes in the fridge. Remove and place in the middle of the paper, curl up all the ends to stop the mirin escaping, pour over fish and fold the corners to completely seal so no air can escape and it steams in its own juices. Place in preheated 180°C oven and bake for 20–25 minutes (depending on size), remove and serve.

Bass with a Middle Eastern Flavour

SERVES 4

- *1 tsp. ground cumin*
- *¼ tsp. cinnamon*
- *4 seabass fillets, skin on*
- *2 tbs. (30ml) olive oil*

Rub the spices over the sea bass and season with sea salt and pepper. Heat oil in a non-stick frying pan and fry skin-side up for 3–4 minutes on each side.

Optional: Delish served with your favourite roasted vegetables.

Batter for Fish

MAKES 2 CUPS

A recipe from the lovely Sharlene Emanuel.

- *½ cup plain flour*
- *½ cup cornflour*
- *1 cup (250ml) very cold water*
- *½ cup (125ml) sunflower oil*

Slowly add the cold water to the flours and keep beating (the secret is in the beating). Beat for at least 5–10 minutes. Then just dip fish of choice into batter and fry in very hot oil for 4 minutes.

Optional: Add herbs and spices to the flours to season.
Ground cumin, turmeric and paprika are particularly nice.

Tip: Using cornflour helps lighten the batter.

Blackened Fish

SERVES 4

- *2 limes, juiced*
- *3 tsp. cajun spice (blackened seasoning)*
- *2 tbs. (30ml) olive oil*
- *4 x 200g snapper fillets*

Combine juice, Cajun seasoning, oil, salt and pepper. Coat fish in mixture and allow to marinate for 20–30 minutes. Preheat BBQ or grill and cook fish on high for 4 minutes each side.

Optional: Serve dolloped with White Bean Puree (see: Sauce, Salsas & Marinades).

Cod Fillets with Sun-Dried Tomatoes

SERVES 4

A recipe from Lisa Darr.

- *1 cup sun dried tomatoes, reserve oil*
- *1 lemon, juiced and zest*
- *2 cloves garlic*
- *4 large cod fillets*

Process tomatoes (with a quarter cup of its oil) lemon juice, zest and garlic. Blend until smooth and season to taste. Place fish in a shallow baking dish and coat well with puree. Cover with foil and allow to marinate in fridge for a minimum of 30 minutes. Preheat oven 160°C and bake covered for 15 minutes or until fish flakes easily. Serve the fish bathed in the *yummmmy* puree.

Crab Won Tons

MAKES APPROX. 16

- *1 cup crab meat*
- *1 tsp. curry powder*
- *1 pkt gow ghee pastry*
- *2 cups (500ml) sunflower oil*

Mix crab and curry powder (add more powder if needed). Place 8 sheets of pastry out at a time. Place a tsp. of crab mixture in the centre of the pastry. Fold over ensuring no air is trapped. Squeeze edges together. Once all mixture is used refrigerate for 20 minutes. Heat oil in a large frying pan and fry for 2–3 minutes or until golden (ensure there is enough oil to cover the won tons).

Optional: These are divine served with our zesty Dipping Sauce (see: Sauces, Salsas & Marinades) and filled with a few shredded vegetables too.

Fish Kebabs

MAKES 12

A recipe from Angie Covino. These are absolutely fabulous!

- *500g firm white fish*
- *2 tbs. (40g) red curry paste*
- *½ bunch fresh coriander, chopped*
- *1 onion, finely chopped*

Mince the fish or process, add curry paste, onion and coriander and mix well. Shape into a sausage shape around a skewer. Set in the fridge for 20 minutes. Cook in a non-stick frying pan.

Optional: Delicious served with a sauce of your choice. e.g yoghurt garlic dip or yoghurt with mint.

Fish Vindaloo

SERVES 4

A recipe from Janelle McCosker.

- *4 x 200g white fish fillets*
- *1 large onion (200g), thinly sliced*
- *¼ cup (80g) vindaloo curry paste*
- *2 tomatoes, coarsely chopped*

Cook fish in a large non-stick frying pan 3–4 minutes each side or until almost cooked. Remove from pan. Add onion and cook over medium heat until softened. Add curry paste, cook stirring until fragrant. Add tomatoes with 1 cup (250ml) of water. Bring to the boil, reduce heat and simmer uncovered for 4 minutes.

Optional: Serve with steamed rice, Asian green vegetables and natural yoghurt if desired.

Gingered Squid

SERVES 4

- *4 medium (about 100g each) cleaned squid hoods*
- *1 tsp. fresh grated ginger*
- *3 tbs. (45ml) oyster sauce*
- *2 tbs. (30ml) sweet chilli sauce*

Place squid on a clean, flat surface. Slide a knife along one side of the squid to open each tube. Lay the pieces flat. Score the squid with diagonal slices. Try to cut through half the thickness (if your scores are too superficial, they won't be apparent when cooked). These cuts will open while cooking and give the squid extra visual interest and texture. Slice squid into smaller, bite-size pieces. Heat a non-stick frying pan to high with ¼ cup of water and bring to boil. Place squid in pan and cook for 1 minute. Drain excess liquid (if any) place back on heat and toss with rest of ingredients season and serve.

Green Curry Salmon Cakes

SERVES 4–6

A delicious recipe by Sharyn Seligman.

- 500g potatoes, peeled and chopped
- 2 tbs. (40g) green curry paste
- ½ cup coarsely chopped coriander
- 415g can pink salmon, drained and flaked

Place potatoes in a large saucepan, cover with cold water and bring to the boil. Boil for 10 minutes or until tender. Drain and mash. Add remaining ingredients, season with sea salt and pepper, shape into patties and cook in a non-stick frying pan until golden brown, approx. 4 minutes each side.

Grilled Chilli Fish

SERVES 4

- 4 x 250g fresh white fish fillets
- 2 limes, juiced
- 2 chillies, seeds and placenta removed
- 3 tbs. brown sugar

Rub fish on both sides with lime juice. Combine remaining juice, sugar and finely chopped chillies and toss with fish. Place on a baking tray and grill in oven for 20 minutes or until cooked through. Turn once.

Tip: This is a great recipe for the BBQ as well!!

Horseradish Baked Salmon

SERVES 4

- *2 slices bread, crusts removed*
- *2 tbs. horseradish cream*
- *2 tsp. thyme*
- *4 thin, skinless salmon steaks*

Grate breadcrumbs, add horseradish and thyme and season with sea salt and pepper, mix well. Place the salmon in a baking dish, press the crumbs onto the fish and bake for 10–12 minutes.

Tip: Frozen bread grates easiest.

Indian Fish Bake

SERVES 6

- *6 fillets of any white fish*
- *4 tbs. garam marsala*
- *3 x 400g cans chopped tomato with herbs*
- *250g Greek yoghurt*

Preheat oven 180°C. Place fish in a baking tray and sprinkle garam marsala evenly. Pour over tomato mixture, season and bake for 1 hour. Remove and drizzle with yoghurt.

Lime Oysters

MAKES 12

- *2 limes, juiced*
- *12 drops tabasco sauce*
- *1 tsp. chopped coriander*
- *12 pacific oysters*

Mix lime, tabasco and coriander. Spoon mixture evenly among the oysters and serve.

Mediterranean Baked Fish

SERVES 6

- *6 fillets of snapper, or any white fish*
- *1 cup basil pesto*
- *1 cup semi dried tomato*
- *1 cup kalmata olives*

Preheat oven 180°C. In a bowl add pesto and coat fish evenly. Place in a baking dish, cover with tomatoes and olives and bake for 15–20 minutes or until fish is cooked through.

Optional: Enjoy the complementary flavours of this dish served with a lovely, fresh salad.

Mexican Oysters

MAKES 12

- *1 avocado, mashed*
- *½ cup sliced jalapenos*
- *½ cup diced tomato*
- *12 pacific oysters*

Mix avocado, jalapenos and tomato. Season with pepper. Place a spoonful of mixture in each oyster and serve.

Oysters with Wasabi Butter

MAKES 12

- *2 tbs. (30g) softened butter*
- *1 lime, juiced and zested*
- *½ tsp. wasabi powder*
- *12 pacific oysters*

Mix butter, lime juice and rind then add wasabi and mix through. Season with cracked black pepper. Add a half a teaspoon to each oyster and grill at high temperature for 2–3 minutes.

Parmesan Crusted Oysters

MAKES 12

- *12 pacific oysters*
- *1 cup shaved parmesan*
- *6 tsp. basil pesto*
- *12 semi dried tomatoes*

Place oysters on a baking tray, add a teaspoon of pesto to each oyster. Evenly spread out parmesan. Place under grill till parmesan is golden brown, garnish with semi dried tomato and season with cracked black pepper.

Peppered Tuna with Four Bean Mix Salad

SERVES 4

- *4 x 250g tuna steaks*
- *500g can four bean mix*
- *2 red onions, diced*
- *¼ bunch freshly chopped coriander*

In a bowl season tuna with cracked black pepper. In a non-stick frying pan, cook tuna till medium rare 1–1½ minutes on each side (longer if you prefer). While tuna is resting, mix remaining ingredients together and season. Place tuna on a nice white plate and serve the 'salady salsa' on top.

Pan Fried Peppered Salmon

SERVES 4

- *4 salmon steaks*
- *2 tbs. lemon pepper seasoning*
- *3 tbs. (45ml) olive oil*
- *3 bunches asparagus*

In a bowl toss salmon with lemon pepper and oil. Add a little salt. Pan fry 4 minutes each side or until cooked to your liking. Blanch asparagus quickly in hot water, then distribute evenly over four plates and top with salmon steaks.

Poached Fish with Tomato Salsa

SERVES 4

This is super yummy, healthy and easy to make.

- *4 fresh white fish fillets*
- *2 limes, juiced*
- *3 punnets cherry tomatoes, cut in half*
- *1 cup fresh coriander, roughly chopped*

In a non-stick frying pan place 4 cups of water with a pinch of salt. Poach fish till cooked through about 10 minutes. Place tomato, coriander and lime juice (with a little zest) in a bowl, mix well and season. Place fish on four separate nice white plates, finish with salsa on top.

Poached Salmon with Lemon Thyme Infused Potatoes

SERVES 4

- ½ cup (125ml) garlic infused olive oil
- 4 kipfler potatoes, sliced
- 4 salmon fillets
- 6 tbs. lemon thyme leaves

In a non-stick frying pan add oil and heat. Add potato and cook till golden. Once cooked, add thyme and remove from heat. Steam salmon for 8–10 minutes or until cooked through by using a steamer or a double boiler. Place potato on the plate, salmon on top and drizzle with the leftover thyme infused oil from the potatoes.

Russian Oysters

MAKES 12

- ½ cup crème fraiche
- 5 tbs. chopped parsley
- 12 oysters
- 6 tsp. caviar

Mix crème fraiche and parsley. Place a spoonful in each oyster, garnish with a tsp. of caviar and serve chilled.

Hint: Essential fatty acids, known as EFAs or the good fats, are Omega-3 fatty acids (among others) which oysters are high in.

Salmon Flan

SERVES 4

Recipe by Jeff Thode.

- 415g tin salmon
- ½ cup (125ml) sour cream
- ½ cup parmesan cheese
- 4 free range eggs, beaten

Preheat oven 180°C. Mix ingredients together and season with pepper. Pour into a baking paper lined pie dish and bake for 30 minutes.

Optional: Add fresh dill to the mix and garnish with it before serving.

Salmon Wrapped in Filo

SERVES 4

- 4 salmon fillets, boned
- 200g baby spinach leaves
- 4 sheets filo pastry
- Olive oil spray

Preheat oven to 180°C. Spray sheets with olive oil and fold in half lengthways. Place salmon on each sheet then cover fish with spinach leaves, season with sea salt and pepper and fold into a parcel. Tuck corners in place, seam side down onto a baking tray. Spray top of pastry with oil and bake in oven for approx 15–20 minutes or until golden brown. Salmon should still be still pink in the centre.

Optional: Delicious served with a Napolitano sauce.

Salt & Pepper Calamari

SERVES 4

- ½ cup (60g) cornflour
- 3 medium (about 100g each) cleaned squid hoods,
  cut into 5mm-thick rings
- ½ cup (125ml) sunflower oil

Place the flour in a plastic bag with 1 tsp. sea salt and 1½ tsp. cracked black pepper and shake. Make sure the calamari has been washed in cool water and dried. Then put it in the bag, coat well. Cook very quickly in a lot of hot oil.

Optional: Salt and pepper amounts should be checked, if you like it very spicy you could add chilli flakes or substitute cracked peppercorns for mixed peppercorns. Serve atop a bed of Asian greens.

Tip: Not all squid are calamari. Calamari is a type of squid and is usually more tender and more expensive.

Seared Thai Salmon

SERVES 2

- 1 tbs. (15ml) macadamia nut oil
- 2 salmon steaks
- 1–2 tbs. Thai red curry paste

Rub curry paste over the salmon. Heat oil in a non-stick frying pan and cook the salmon for 4–5 minutes each side, turning only once, until cooked through.

Optional: This is delicious served with Ginger & Broccoli Sautéed Salad (see Salads).

Seared Tuna with Green Beans & Poached Egg

SERVES 4

A recipe from Dan Primmer. A variation of Niçoise.

- ½ cup (125ml) garlic infused olive oil
- 4 x 150g tuna steaks
- 48 green beans toped 'n' tailed
- 4 free range eggs poached

Heat a non-stick frying pan, add half of the oil and sear tuna till medium rare. While tuna is cooking place beans in pot of salted water blanch beans till bright green (about 30 seconds). Divide evenly on four, plates place tuna on top and poached eggs. Place poached eggs on top of beans, season with cracked black pepper and salt and drizzle remaining oil on each plate.

Sizzling Prawns

SERVES 4

- 500g raw king prawns, peeled
- 2 red capsicums, largely diced
- ¾ cup (200ml) Teriyaki sauce
- 2 red onions diced

Separate ingredients into four lots. Heat four sizzling plates, sauté onion first and capsicums add a little water instead of oil to cook. Add prawns and cook till colored then add sauce, season and serve.

Summer Fish Cakes

SERVES 4

- *500g white fish fillets, cooked and flaked*
- *4 tbs. freshly chopped coriander*
- *2 tbs. (40g) pad Thai paste*
- *2 cups mashed sweet potato (kumara)*

Mix all ingredients together. Combine fish, coriander and paste and mash together. Roll mixture into approx. ten cakes. Heat a non-stick frying pan and cook both sides till golden brown.

Optional: Roll in sesame seeds for a lovely crunch.

Swordfish Fried in Sage Olive Oil

SERVES 4

- *3 tbs. (45ml) olive oil*
- *2 tbs. sage leaves*
- *2 tsp. grated lemon rind*
- *4 thin swordfish steaks*

Heat oil in a large frying pan over medium-high heat. Add sage, lemon rind and pepper and cook for 2 minutes or until the sage is crisp. Add swordfish to the pan and cook for 1 minute on each side or until almost cooked through. Serve the swordfish drizzled with the sage oil.

Tartare Sauce

MAKES 1 CUP

- 1 cup (260g) mayonnaise
- 1 tsp. capers
- 1 tbs. gherkin relish
- 1 tbs. chopped parsley

Mix all ingredients together. Serve chilled with any seafood, it's delish!

Teriyaki Salmon

SERVES 2

- 2 skinless salmon fillets
- 1 small onion, sliced
- 3 garlic cloves, halved & thinly sliced
- ½ cup (125ml) teriyaki sauce

Place salmon fillets on a large sheet of foil. Lay sliced onions and garlic on top. Fold sides of foil to create a dish, gently pour teriyaki sauce over salmon, and fold foil to create a sealed packet. Marinate in the fridge for 30 minutes. Place salmon packets on baking tray and in a preheated 180°C oven, cook for 30 minutes. Check by opening packet very carefully as it contains hot steam.

Hint: To intensify flavours, marinate salmon for at least 30 minutes before cooking.

Tuna with Anchovy Paste

SERVES 4

- 4 anchovy fillets in oil
- 3 cloves garlic, sliced
- 4 tuna fillets, thinly sliced
- 2 tsp. butter, melted

Heat a non-stick frying pan, pour in some of the anchovy oil and add garlic. Brush tuna with butter and place in the pan. Count to ten, turn and count to ten again, spread the anchovy paste on the fish and serve.

Tip: Fabulous with boiled potatoes or salad.

Warm Cajun Fish Salad

SERVES 2

- 1 cup green beans, top 'n' tailed
- 2 fresh white fish fillets
- 2 tbs. Cajun spice
- 1 medium mango, sliced

Steam green beans, allow to cool. Coat one side of fish in Cajun spice and pan fry spice side down for 3 minutes. Coat remaining side, flip and cook for a further 3 minutes. Arrange on a plate with green beans and add mango slices to garnish. Sensational!

Whole Sole

SERVES 2

A recipe from Miranda Kerr.

- *1 whole lemon sole (or any deep water fish)*
- *1 sweet potato (kumara), peeled*
- *2 cups baby spinach*
- *2 slices haloumi*

Place fish on a foil lined tray and grill under a medium/hot heat 5–6 minutes on either side. Meanwhile steam and mash one sweet potato. Blanch some baby spinach leaves and grill haloumi. Neatly arrange on a plate to serve.

Optional: Before serving drizzle with freshly squeezed lemon juice.

Homemade Pasta

*Making homemade pasta is truly an amazing experience.
I was 40 when I had my first attempt. Learning how to knead, roll,
flour and cook, then listening to the 'oohs' and 'aahs' from my family
as they ate it, was incredibly satisfying.
I don't know what it is about making pasta from scratch...
But I kind of felt like I'd achieved something truly special!*

Kim McCosker

Tips for Homemade Pasta

Cooking Pasta: Pasta must be cooked in copious salted water. Gradually add pasta and continue to cook at a boil until pasta is "al dente" or slightly firm to the bite. Pasta floats to the top of the water while cooking, so stir occasionally to keep it cooking evenly. Drain in a colander.

Dry Pasta: Requires 6 minutes of cooking

Fresh Pasta: Requires 3–5 minutes of cooking

Salt : Water Ratio: 1tsp. salt : 1 litre boiling water.

Pasta : Water Ratio: The ratio is 1.5 litres : 100g dry pasta

Homemade Pasta

SERVES 1

- 1 cup (100g) Italian '00' flour
- 1 free range egg (59g), beaten

Place the flour directly onto a clean bench so that it forms a mound. Add a pinch of salt, then make a large hollow in the centre and pour in the egg. Use your hands to bring the mass together, start to stir the egg, gradually drawing in the flour until you have a dough. Knead the dough for 10–15 minutes, until it is smooth and quite elastic. Allow dough to rest for an hour, covered. Roll dough using a rolling pin, but it's easier with a pasta machine. A small one with a handle is all you need. Begin with the largest setting on the machine. Flatten the dough into a disc and begin to feed it through the rollers with one hand while turning the handle with the other. Re-flour and roll again, roll twice on each setting until you reach the second or last setting (depending on what type of pasta you are making) re-flouring after each roll.

Hint: Kneading the dough well is very important to prevent it tearing.

Agnolotti

MAKES 50

- 4 cups (100g) Italian '00' flour
- 4 free range eggs (59g), beaten

Make as in Homemade Pasta but rest your pasta sheets to dry a little. Using a 6cm cutter, cut out little circles. Place a small amount of filling (½ a tsp.) in the centre of each circle, wet edges and fold the circle in half. Press along the edges to seal the filling inside (ensuring no air bubbles).

Fettucine

SERVES 4

- *4 cups (100g) Italian '00' flour*
- *4 free range eggs (59g), beaten*

Make as in Homemade Pasta, rest your pasta sheets to dry a little. Change the pasta machine setting or attachment to fettuccine. Choose the first pasta sheet made. Feed through the machine to cut into fettuccine.

Lasagna

SERVES 4

- *4 cups (100g) Italian '00' flour*
- *4 free range eggs (59g), beaten*

Make as in Homemade Pasta. As you make each sheet, cut into rectangular pieces. These are lovely used immediately in your family's favourite lasagna or if you have leftovers, layer sheets separately on a baking paper lined tray, cover with cling wrap and freeze.

Ravioli

MAKES 50

- *4 cups (100g) Italian '00' flour*
- *4 free range eggs (59g), beaten*

Make pasta sheets as above. Roll the pasta dough one sheet at a time and lay on a floured flat surface. On half of the pasta sheet place teaspoons of the mixture in two rows, evenly placed about 6cm apart. Brush between the rows with a little diluted egg wash. Now fold the other half of the sheet over the mounds of filling and carefully press down around each one, careful to remove air pockets. Using either a biscuit or ravioli cutter (or even a knife) cut into squares or round shapes. Sprinkle with a little flour and place on tea towels while you finish the rest of the dough and filling. When you are ready to eat, cook in boiling salted water until the pasta floats.

Tip: For filled pasta such as ravioli, cut and fill the pasta sheet as you go rather than rolling out all the dough.

Tortellini

MAKES 50

- *4 cups (100g) Italian '00' flour*
- *4 free range eggs (59g), beaten*

Roll the pasta dough one sheet at a time and lay on a floured flat surface. Cut into 7 x 7cm squares. Place a tsp. of filling in the centre of the sheet, wet the edges with water and fold in half to form a triangle. Gently press to remove air bubbles and seal edges well. Take the furthest edges and pinch together. Lay on a baking paper lined tray, when the bottom layer full, line again with baking paper and repeat layering process. Cook in salted boiling water when needed.

Potato Gnocchi

SERVES 4

- 4 potatoes, washed, peeled
- 1 free range egg, lightly whisked
- 2 cups (300g) plain flour (extra for dusting)
- ¼ cup finely grated parmesan cheese

Peel potatoes and microwave on high for 5-6 minutes or until soft, remove and cool. Transfer to a bowl and use a potato masher to mash until smooth. Season with salt and pepper. Add the egg and stir with a wooden spoon until combined. Add half the flour and parmesan and stir until combined. Add the remaining flour, in two more batches, until well combined and a firm dough forms (if dough is too soft, add more flour.) Turn onto a lightly floured surface and knead until smooth. Line a baking tray with non-stick baking paper. Divide dough into 4 equal portions. Roll each portion into a long 30cm log. Cut into 2cm wide pieces. Use a lightly floured fork and press into the gnocchi a couple of times to make indentations (which helps the sauce stick) and chill on a baking tray for 10 minutes. Bring a saucepan of salted water to the boil over medium heat. Add ¼ of the gnocchi and cook for 3 minutes or until they rise to the surface. Use a slotted spoon to drain and transfer to a bowl. Cover with foil to keep warm. Repeat, with the remaining gnocchi.

Optional: Make a double batch and freeze until required.

Tip: Flavour for a change, replace potato with 2 (about 800g) orange sweet potato (kumara) and increase the flour to 2½ cups or increase grated parmesan to ½ cup (40g) and add ½ cup finely chopped fresh basil to the flour.

Ricotta Gnocchi

SERVES 4

- *250g fresh ricotta, well drained*
- *1 free range egg yolk, separated*
- *⅔ cup (55g) finely grated parmesan*
- *⅓ cup (50g) plain flour*

Combine ricotta, yolk, parmesan and season. Fold in the flour. Using a teaspoon, roll the mixture into balls and place on a paper lined baking tray. Cover with cling film and pop in the fridge. When ready, bring a large saucepan of salted water to the boil. Cook gnocchi balls in batches for 2 minutes or until they rise to the surface. Use a slotted spoon to transfer to a dry tea towel.

Optional: These are super tasty in soups, broths or served with your favourite pasta sauce.

Roman Style Gnocchi

SERVES 4

- *1 ltr. milk*
- *250g polenta*
- *2 tbs. fresh thyme leaves*
- *⅔ cup (55g) finely grated parmesan*

In a large saucepan bring milk to boil. Reduce heat and gradually add polenta whilst whisking continuously. Continue to stir for 10 minutes or until cooked and thick. Remove from heat and stir in thyme and cheese (reserving some for serving). Spread mixture onto a paper lined baking tray and cool in the fridge. When set, use a small cookie cutter to cut until all mixture is used. Using a greased baking dish, layer gnocchi discs so they slightly overlap. Pour over your family's favourite Napolitano sauce, top with reserved parmesan and bake in a 180°C oven for 10–15 minutes or until cheese is golden.

Flavoured Pasta

As introduced by Angela Covino
a talented Chef and beautiful Italian Mamma to boot!

Beetroot:	Add 2 tbs. cooked and blended beetroot, use 1 large egg.
Black Olive:	Serve with tomato based sauces.
Chilli:	Add 1 tsp. chilli powder to the dough. A beautiful match with the creaminess of an Alfredo.
Garlic:	Add 3 tbs. finely ground herbs. Garlic pasta excels with a tomato sauce or pesto.
Curry:	Add 1 tsp. to the dough. Serve with coconut milk or chicken stock based sauces.
Herb:	Add 3 tbs. finely ground herbs. Delicious served with tomato based sauces.
Lemon:	Add 2 tbs. lemon juice. This pasta is great for chicken or seafood dishes, and excellent in cold pasta salads.
Pumpkin:	Add 2 tbs. cooked and mashed pumpkin, use 1 large egg.
Rosemary:	Add 2 tbs. cooked and mashed pumpkin, use 1 large egg.
Saffron:	Soak 1 sachet of powder saffron in 2 tbs. hot water for 15 minutes. This pasta is outstanding with all seafood, white wine sauces and subtle cheeses.
Spinach:	Blend 150g frozen leaf spinach cooked and squeezed well. Season and use 1 free range egg instead of two.
Tomato:	Add 2 tbs. tomato puree or sundried tomato paste and use 1 large free range egg (70g) instead of two. Try serving with a light, creamy Alfredo.
Wasabi:	Add 1 tbs. wasabi paste. Like saffron, it pairs well with most Asian flavours.
Whole Wheat:	Use sifted whole wheat flour instead of '00' flour.

Pasta Fillings

*Dreams are not something to **wait for**, they are something to **work for**.*

Author Unknown

Chicken & Lemongrass

ENOUGH FOR 50 PARCELS

- 300g cooked free range chicken meat, finely chopped
- 2cm piece lemongrass
- ½ tsp. fresh ginger
- 100g ricotta

Blend altogether in a food processor until quite pasty.

Prawn Curry

ENOUGH FOR 50 PARCELS

- 500g green prawns, peeled and deveined
- 100g crème fraiche
- ½ lemon, juiced
- 1 tsp. red curry paste

Blend prawn meat in a food processor. Fold through remaining ingredients.

Roasted Garlic & Basil

ENOUGH FOR 50 PARCELS

- 4 cloves garlic, roasted
- 50g pecorino cheese, finely grated
- 100g ricotta
- 8 fresh basil leaves, chopped

Mash roasted garlic and mix in remaining ingredients.

Hint: To roast garlic, peel off the outer layers of the bulb, leaving just a single layer intact. Using a knife cut off ½ cm of the top of the clove. Place on a baking tray and drizzle with olive oil. Cover with foil and bake in a 180°C oven for 30–35 minutes.

Roasted Pumpkin & Pepita

ENOUGH FOR 50 PARCELS

- 200g roasted pumpkin, cooled
- 100g fetta cheese
- 1 tbs. garlic, gourmet garden
- 2 tbs. toasted pepita seeds, chopped

Mash together the first 3 ingredients then fold in pepita seeds.

Tip: Make double the quantity and freeze half for another quick and easy family meal.

Spinach & Fetta

ENOUGH FOR 50 PARCELS

- *500g bunch silverbeet*
- *1 onion, finely diced*
- *1 tsp. nutmeg*
- *300g ricotta*

Remove silverbeet stalks, finely chop and steam until wilted, squeeze out excess water. Fry onion gently in a frypan until translucent. Mix silverbeet, onion and ricotta together and add nutmeg, sea salt and pepper for a sensational pasta filling.

Wild Mushroom

ENOUGH FOR 50 PARCELS

- *500g wild mushrooms, sliced*
- *½ cup of spinach*
- *200g goats cheese*
- *2 tbs. pine nuts, toasted and chopped*

Pan fry mushrooms over high heat until water evaporates. Meanwhile steam spinach for 3-4 minutes and cool. Finely chop mushrooms and spinach and mix together with goats cheese and pine nuts.

Pasta Sauces

My relationships are a mirror of myself.

Deepak Chopra

Broccoli & Pine Nut Pasta Sauce

SERVES 4

- *400g broccoli*
- *100g pine nuts, toasted*
- *3 tbs. (45ml) olive oil*
- *2 cloves garlic, thinly sliced*

Separate broccoli into stem and florets and boil in salted water for 4 - 6 minutes, or until tender. Drain all, reserving ¼ cup of liquid. Add to broccoli, pine nuts, olive oil and garlic and mix in the reserved water. Serve warm mixed through a short pasta like penne.

Optional: Sprinkle with parmesan, add 2 anchovies.

Chilli & Garlic

SERVES 2

Recipe by Angie Covino.

- *3 tbs.(45ml) olive oil*
- *2 small red chillies, seeded*
- *2 cloves garlic, crushed*
- *1 tbs. flat leaf parsley*

Cook the pasta until al dente, drain and reserve ¼ cup of the water. Heat the olive oil, cook the chilli's and garlic until fragrant. Toss in pasta and reserved water (just enough to wet the pasta).

Chilli Infused Crab Sauce

SERVES 2

Recipe by Spud Moore.

- ½ cup blue swimmer crab meat
- 2 tbs. (30ml) chilli infused oil
- 1 tbs. (15ml) lemon juice
- ½ cup fresh peas

In a non-stick frying pan, heat chilli oil until warm. Fold through all other ingredients and serve.

Suggested pasta: Linguine, spaghetti and flavoured pastas such as saffron, tomato and lemon myrtle.

Eggplant & Tomato Sauce

SERVES 4

- 3 medium eggplants, diced
- 500g very ripe tomatoes
- 3 tbs. (45ml) garlic infused olive oil
- 2 tbs. fresh basil

Put eggplants in colander, sprinkle with sea salt and set aside for 30 minutes (doing this leaches out the bitterness from the eggplant). Meanwhile dip tomatoes in boiling water for 10 seconds, remove skins, and chop coarsely. Fry in oil until they disintegrate, rinse eggplants to remove salt and pat dry. Add to tomatoes and cook until eggplants are soft. This sauce results in a chunky consistency and is a beautiful accompaniment to freshly made fettuccine.

Optional: Garnish with 3–4 tbs. fresh ricotta or parmesan cheese.

Fiery Red Pepper Sauce

SERVES 4

- *6 red capsicums, halved and deseeded*
- *4 tbs. (60ml) garlic infused olive oil*
- *2 large red chillies, chopped*
- *4 ripe tomatoes, chopped*

Cut capsicums into medium chunks. Heat oil in a non-stick frying pan, add capsicum and chillies and cook for 1 minute or until golden. Stir in tomatoes, simmer and reduce to a chunky type salsa.

Suggested pasta: Spinach fettuccine, garnished with fresh basil leaves.

Napoletana

SERVES 4

Recipe by Spud Moore.

- *1 onion, finely chopped*
- *3 cloves garlic, crushed*
- *4½ cups of diced Italian/Roma tomatoes*
- *¼ cup fresh basil leaves, coarsely torn*

Cook onion and garlic in a non-stick frypan. Add tomatoes undrained to pan and bring to boil. Lower heat and allow to simmer uncovered for 20 minutes or until slightly reduced. Stir in fresh basil and serve on top of pasta.

Optional: Serve with grated parmesan cheese.

Suggested pasta: Spaghetti, Ravioli, Agnolotti.

Prawn & Lemon Linguine

SERVES 4

- 350g linguine
- 300g fresh green prawns
- 1 lemon, juice and zest
- ½ cup (125ml) of cream

Cook pasta. Meanwhile heat a non-stick frying pan, add lemon juice, zest and prawns and gently cook for 3–4 minutes or until prawns start to turn orange in colour. Season and stir in cream, allow to bubble for 1 minute, simmer until sauce slightly reduces. Drain linguine and return to the pan with the sauce, tossing to coat.

Sage & Pecan Sauce

SERVES 6

- 1½ tbs. butter
- ¼ cup chopped pecans
- 3 tbs. freshly chopped sage leaves
- 250ml cooking cream

Melt butter in a non-stick frying pan over medium heat. Add pecans and stir until slightly darker and fragrant, about 3 minutes. Using a slotted spoon, transfer pecans to a small bowl. Add sage and sauté for about 30 seconds or until fragrant. Add cream. Stir until cream has melted and is warm. Add pecans, stir and serve.

Scallop, Asparagus & Chilli Sauce

SERVES 2

- 6 scallops, roe off
- ½ bunch fresh asparagus trimmed into 2cm pieces
- ½ red chilli, with seeds removed and finely chopped
- ½ tsp. lemon zest

In a non-stick fry pan, seal scallops and put aside. Blanch off asparagus and put aside. Fry chilli in a little bit of water, return scallops and asparagus. Add warm pasta of choice and lemon zest, toss to combine and serve.

Suggested pasta: Angel hair, spaghetti, linguine.

Tip: To blanch any vegetable, plunge it into boiling water. Boil for 1–2 minutes, remove and drop into ice water. This shocks the vegetable and seals in its natural colour. If you don't, it will continue to cook internally and will often turn mushy and a grayish green in colour.

Smoked Salmon & Blue Cheese

SERVES 2

Recipe by Spud Moore.

- 100g smoked salmon, coarsely chopped
- 2 tbs. (30g) blue cheese
- ½ cup (125ml) cream
- 2 sprigs of chives, chopped

Add cream and crumbled blue cheese to a non-stick frypan on medium heat. Stir until just boiled, add cooked pasta and fold in salmon and chives. Serve.

Walnut & Caper Pesto

SERVES 2

- ⅔ cup (185ml) garlic infused olive oil
- ⅔ cup (85g) walnuts
- 1 tbs. freshly chopped parsley
- 2 tbs. capers

Blend ingredients in food processor to a chunky texture. A flavoursome sauce that can be mixed with spinach tagliatelle for a delicious, healthy meal!

Vine Ripened Tomato & Olive Sauce

SERVES 2

Recipe by Spud Moore.

- 2 large vine ripened tomatoes, diced
- ¼ cup pitted kalamata olives, cut in half – reserve liquid
- 1 big handful of rocket leaves
- ¼ cup caramelised onion jam

Place tomatoes and reserved olive liquid into a non-stick frypan, season with salt and pepper. Lightly warm tomatoes, add olives, stir lightly and turn heat off. Toss rocket and carmelised onion through warm pasta of choice and lastly fold in tomatoes and olives.

Suggested pasta: Gnocchi, penne.

Vegetarian & Legumes

Each year, around 98% of each one of us is made up of
BRAND NEW CELLS.
So, even if you are feeling overweight or unhealthy today,
there is no reason that you have to stay that way!

Deepak Chopra

Aubergine & Sweet Potato Curry

SERVES 4

This is really yummy!

- *2 onions, peeled and sliced*
- *1 aubergine (eggplant), chopped into 2cm pieces*
- *1 medium to large size sweet potatoes (kumara), peeled & chopped into large chunks*
- *350g korma mildly spiced organic sauce*

Simmer onion in water until tender. Remove from pan and set aside. In a non-stick fry pan, fry aubergines until browned evenly. Return onions to pan with sweet potato and korma sauce. Fill half the empty jar with water and add to pan. Simmer for 20–30 minutes until the potato and aubergine are tender.

Optional: Serve with rice and pappadums.

Tip: There are various names for the aubergine among different countries. Aubergine is used in the United Kingdom. 'Eggplant' is used in the United States, Canada, Australia & New Zealand. It is assumed that the name came from the fact that prior to 1700's the main European cultivation of this vegetable were white or yellowish and roughly the size of a goose egg … Hence an 'Eggplant.'

Baked Pumpkin & Sage Flan

SERVES 6

This is super yummy, TRY IT!

- *250g butternut pumpkin, peeled, diced and roasted*
- *500g fresh ricotta*
- *3 free range eggs, lightly beaten*
- *3 tbs. fresh sage leaves*

Preheat oven 200°C. Line a quiche dish with baking paper and lay ¾ of the roasted pumpkin on it. Combine ricotta and eggs in a bowl and stir well. Using a spatula, pour mixture over pumpkin, sprinkle generously with sage and season. Dollop remaining pumpkin around the top of the flan. Bake for 35-40 minutes or until firm and golden. Allow to cool before removing.

Optional: These can also be made in muffin trays, reduce baking time to 15 minutes or until the pies are firm and golden.

BBQ Mushroom & Zucchini

SERVES 2–4

- *4 cups sliced mushrooms*
- *4 zucchinis, sliced*
- *½ cup (125ml) garlic infused olive oil*
- *1 tbs. Cajun spice*

On a hot BBQ plate add the oil and sauté mushrooms and zucchini. Sprinkle with cajun spice, gently toss together and season with a little salt. Remove from heat. Serve.

Bean Stir-Fry

SERVES 4

- 1 tbs. (15g) butter
- 300g green beans, top 'n' tailed
- 100g bean sprouts, washed and drained
- 2 tsp. paprika

Heat the butter in a wok, add the green beans and stir-fry gently for 4 minutes. Push the beans to the side of the wok, turn the heat up and add the bean sprouts. Stir-fry for 2 minutes. Mix the beans and sprouts together adding the paprika, a little salt and plenty of black pepper, stir-fry for 1 more minute and serve.

Optional: Serve with some lovely couscous or brown rice.

Beetroot & Goats Cheese Risotto

SERVES 4

- 2 beetroots, trimmed
- 2 cups (500ml) vegetable stock
- 100g goats cheese
- 1 cup (185g) arborio rice

Boil the beetroot whole in plenty of salted water for 50-60 minutes or until cooked through. Drain, reserving 2 cups (500ml) of liquid. Cool the beetroot, peel and dice. Combine the reserved liquid with the stock and bring to a gentle simmer. Add the rice and stir gently until liquid is almost evaporated. The risotto should maintain a rapid simmer. After 10 minutes add the beetroot and continue stirring until the rice is al dente and has the consistency of wet porridge. Season to taste. Serve the risotto crumbled with goats cheese.

Optional: Serve drizzled with lemon juice.

Broad Beans with Sesame Seeds

SERVES 6

- 500g broad beans, fresh or frozen, peeled
- 2 tbs. sesame seeds
- 2 tbs. (30g) butter
- 1 tbs. (15ml) lemon juice

Cook the beans in boiling salted water until tender, 8-15 minutes depending if frozen or fresh. While the beans are cooking, toast the sesame seeds until lightly brown. Drain the beans and put the butter in the pan. When melted, add lemon juice and pepper. Stir the beans through the butter, serve hot sprinkled with sesame seeds.

Tips: Broad beans are a good source of calcium, so are particularly valuable to those who do not eat dairy products.

Bouquet of Garni

MAKES 1

- 4 parsley stems
- 4 thyme
- 4 bay leaves
- 4 black peppercorns

Tie the herbs with unwaxed kitchen string. Place on a piece of muslin, add peppercorns and secure with more string. Using this with a slice of lemon, apple or chilli (depending on how hot you like it) will almost satisfy the 6 tastes of Ayurveda in one meal!

Tip: Bouquet garni is French for "garnished bouquet." It's a bundle of aromatic herbs with string (making it easy to remove after cooking) which you can add to casseroles, stews or soups for extra flavour and fragrance.

Cheese Polenta

MAKES 12

- 2 cups (500ml) vegetable stock
- 375g polenta
- ⅓ cup (85ml) cream
- ½ cup grated parmesan cheese

Place 2 cups of water and stock in a large saucepan. Bring to the boil over high heat. Gradually add the polenta in a thin steady stream, stirring constantly with a wooden spoon until well incorporated. Reduce the heat to low and cook, stirring, for 2 minutes or until the mixture thickens and the polenta is soft. Remove from heat. Add the cream and parmesan and stir until well combined. Taste and season with salt and pepper.

Optional: This is delicious served with Herbed or Sautéed Mushrooms (see: Vegetables).

Chickpea Patties

MAKES 12

- 500g sweet potato (kumara), peeled and chopped
- 2 x 400g cans chickpeas
- ½ cup finely chopped spring onion
- ¼ cup (80g) curry paste

Place kumara into a microwave-safe plate in a single layer. Cover. Microwave for 3–5 minutes on high or until just tender. Drain. Transfer to a bowl. Add chickpeas. Mash mixture until almost smooth. Stir through remaining ingredients, season with sea salt and pepper. Mix until well combined. Using damp hands, form mixture into patties. Heat a large non-stick frying pan over medium heat. Cook patties for 3–4 minutes each side or until golden and heated through.

Classic Cheese Fondue

SERVES 4

- 1 cup (250ml) dry white wine
- 600g gruyere cheese
- 1½ tsp. cornflour
- 1 pinch nutmeg

Place fondue pot on medium heat. Add wine and bring to boil, reduce heat, add cheese and stir in a figure eight motion until cheese melts. It should take five minutes or so to melt. Add cornflour and stir. Mixture should be thick enough to coat a piece of bread.

Hint: Fondue originated in Switzerland as a way of using up hardened cheese. Deriving from the French verb fondre, meaning 'to melt' ... We love it as a real way to share a meal with family and friends, it's social, fun and above all DELICIOUS!

Crisp Peppered Tofu

SERVES 2

- 2 tbs. Szechuan peppercorns
- 1 cup rice flour
- 250g block firm tofu, cubed
- 3–4 tbs. sesame oil

Toast and pound the peppercorns in a mortar and pestle. Add to rice flour, coat tofu before frying in hot sesame oil until nice and crisp on the outside.

Optional: Can marinate tofu cubes in Tamari before coating for a different flavour. This is lovely served atop a bed of steamed Asian greens.

Corn Pancakes

MAKES 8

- *4 cobs of corn, cooked*
- *4 spring onions, finely chopped*
- *2 tbs. self raising flour*
- *1 free range egg*

When cool, remove corn kernels with a sharp knife. Combine corn, spring onion, flour and egg mashing lightly with a potato masher. Cover and chill for one hour. Heat a non-stick pan, drop 2 tbs. of corn mixture in. Cook over a medium heat for 2–3 minutes each side.

Optional: Delicious served with mashed avocado and sweet chilli sauce. You can add 1 tsp. each of curry powder & soy sauce for extra zing!!

Cumin Flavoured Lentils

SERVES 4

- *1 cup (170g) of green lentils*
- *½ tbs. ground cumin*
- *¼ tsp. salt*
- *¼ tsp. pepper*

Mix all these ingredients in a pot with 2½ cups of water. Bring to the boil and cook for 10 minutes. Watch water levels as you may need to add a little more. Reduce heat to low and simmer for 15–20 minutes.

Optional: Serve them as a side dish or serve them on top of rice as a meal.

Eggplant Slice

SERVES 4

- *2 tbs. (30ml) garlic infused olive oil*
- *2 large eggplants, sliced 1cm thick*
- *4 cups sliced bocconcini*
- *6 Roma tomatoes, sliced*

In a non-stick frying pan, heat oil and fry eggplant until golden. In a shallow baking dish place eggplant and layer with sliced tomato, followed by bocconcini. Season with cracked black pepper and sea salt. Grill until the cheese melts.

Optional: Serve with a fresh green salad.

Healthy Pie Base

MAKES 1

- *1 cup wholemeal breadcrumbs*
- *¼ cup millet meal*
- *½ tsp. onion powder*
- *1 tbs. (15ml) sunflower oil*

Preheat oven to 180°C. Combine ingredients in a food processor and process until it begins to stick together. Lightly grease a pie dish and press down over base and sides. Cook for approximately 15 minutes before adding your choice of filling.

Lentil Patties

MAKES 15

- 1 cup (170g) brown lentils
- ½ cup bulgar wheat
- 2 free range eggs
- 3 tbs. Gourmet Garden Moroccan blend

Boil lentils in 2½ cups (625ml) water for 30 minutes or until soft. Add the bulgur and cover, allowing it to absorb the remaining water. Add remaining ingredients and roll into balls. In a non-stick frying pan cook for 2–3 minutes each side or until crisp and brown.

Optional: Delicious served with Mint Salsa (see: Sauces, Salsas & Marinades).

Mini Pumpkin Bake

MAKES 4

- 4 mini pumpkins
- 3 cups couscous
- 1 jar of mixed char-grilled vegetables
- 12 asparagus spears, stems removed and chopped

Preheat oven 180°C. Remove tops of pumpkins and remove seeds. Place lids and bases on a baking tray with grease proof paper. Drain jar, reserving oil. Drizzle oil over pumpkins, season and cook for 20 minutes or until soft. In a large stainless steel bowl, add couscous and three cups of boiling water. Cover with cling film for 10 minutes to cook couscous via steaming process. Add vegetables and mix. Place pumpkin in the middle of a nice white plate, fill with mixture and serve.

Mushroom Stroganoff

SERVES 2

Recipe by Kate Henderson.

- *250ml creme fraiche or sour cream*
- *8 peeled mushrooms, sliced*
- *1 tsp. fresh lemon juice*
- *1 finely chopped onion*

Place onion and mushrooms in non-stick pan and cook down until soft and onions begin to brown. Reduce heat, add creme fraiche and stir well, add a splash of lemon juice and season with sea salt and black pepper to taste.

Optional: Serve spooned over a jacket potato or with rice and peas.

Pumpkin & Lentil Curry

SERVES 4

Recipe from Susan Hay that is simply scrumptious!

- *2 tbs. (40g) red curry paste*
- *400ml can coconut milk*
- *250g pumpkin, peeled and chopped*
- *1 cup (170g) green lentils*

In a non-stick frying pan, add paste and fry over medium heat until fragrant. Pour in coconut milk and ½ cup of water and mix to combine. Add pumpkin and simmer for 25 minutes or until almost soft. Add lentils, cover and simmer until soft.

Optional: Serve with rice and chapattis.

Rice Crusted Quiche Base

MAKES 1

- 1 free range egg
- 3 cups (550g) long grain rice, cooked and warm
- 3 tbs. finely grated parmesan cheese

Preheat oven 170°C. Line a quiche dish with baking paper. In a bowl lightly whisk the egg. Add rice and parmesan and mix to combine. Lightly press the mix into the base of the dish. Bake for 15 minutes or until just starting to turn golden brown.

Optional: Fill with your favourite quiche filling. Remember the easy quiche recipe from 4 ingredients cleverly combining just eggs, sour cream and your fillings of choice!

Scorched Corn Couscous

SERVES 6

- 2 cups dry couscous
- 2 tsp. dry vegetable stock
- 3 cooked corn on the cobs
- 3 spring onions, sliced

Heat a grill plate or BBQ until hot, place cobs on turning frequently until all the corn is scorched. Slice kernels from the cob and set aside. Place couscous and stock in a large bowl, stir in 2 cups boiling water, cover and stand for 5 minutes. Meanwhile pan fry spring onions for 2–3 minutes, adding corn in the final minute. Fluff couscous before seasoning with pepper and stirring in corn kernels and spring onions.

Sesame Crusted Tofu & Capsicum Kebabs

MAKES 4

- *250g firm tofu, cut into small cubes*
- *2 tbs. sesame seeds*
- *3 red capsicums, chopped into chunks*
- *4 tbs. (60ml) sweet chilli sauce*

Coat tofu and capsicum in sesame seeds. Thread capsicum and tofu alternately onto soaked skewers. Grill turning, turning frequently for 6–8 minutes or until sesame seeds are beginning to brown. Transfer to a plate and serve with sweet chilli sauce to dip.

Tip: An alternative to soaking skewers is to keep them in your freezer and pull out when needed.

Sweet Chilli Corn Cakes

SERVES 4

- *4 large potatoes, peeled and chopped*
- *2 corn cobs. kernels removed*
- *1 free range egg, beaten*
- *¼ cup (62ml) sweet chilli sauce*

Bring to boil 4 cups water in a saucepan. Add potatoes, bring to the boil, reduce heat, cover and cook for approximately 6–8 minutes or until tender. Add corn kernels and boil for a further 2–3 minutes. Drain. Add egg and sauce and shape into 8 cakes. Heat a non-stick frying pan and cook for 2–3 minutes each side or until golden brown.

Optional: Delicious served dolloped with Sweet Chilli Mayonnaise (see: Sauces, Salsas & Marinades).

Vegetarian Tagine

SERVES 4

- 3 tbs. Gourmet Garden Moroccan paste
- 8 dried figs, quartered
- 200g sweet potato (kumara), peeled and diced
- 300g chickpeas, tinned

Place paste, figs and kumara into a large non-stick frying pan with one cup of water. Cover and simmer for 4 minutes. Add chickpeas and simmer for a further 6 minutes or until tender.

Optional: Serve with couscous and Minted Yoghurt (see: Sauces, Salsas and Marinades). For further goodness, add mixed vegies e.g., pumpkin, capsicum, beans, cauliflower, zucchini ... Whatever you have and whatever your family will eat!

Tip: A tagine is a type of dish found in North African cuisines of Algeria, Morocco and Tunisia, which is named after the special pot in which it is cooked. Most tagines involve slow simmering, resulting in tender meat and aromatic vegetables and sauces.

Desserts

Be Yourself ... Everyone else is taken!

Anonymous

Almond Cream

MAKES 1 CUP

- *125g blanched almonds*
- *⅓ cup (85ml) apple juice*

Place both ingredients in a food processor and blend until nice and creamy. This is delicious spooned over fresh fruit.

Apple & Date Spring Rolls

SERVES 4

- *100g dried apple, chopped*
- *16 pitted dates, dried and chopped*
- *8 spring roll wrappers*
- *1 cup (250ml) sunflower oil*

Soak apple and dates in boiling water until tender. Drain, mix and then cool in fridge. Spoon equal amounts of apple mixture onto each spring roll wrapper. Fold up the spring roll. Shallow fry in hot oil for 2 minutes or until golden brown.

Optional: Dust generously with icing sugar to serve.

Apples with Lemon & Honey

SERVES 2

A simple, straightforward, healthy dessert.

- *2 apples*
- *2 tsp. honey*
- *1 lemon*

Slice the apples into thin circles. Mix 1 tsp. lemon zest and juice with honey and drizzle over apple.

Baked Apple with Cinnamon

SERVES 4

- *4 green apples*
- *2 tsp. cinnamon sugar*
- *4 tbs. (60g) butter*
- *1 cup (170g) organic raisins*

Preheat oven 180°C. Scoop out the core from top of the apple, leaving a well. Do not cut all the way through. Stuff each apple with equal parts of raisins, butter and cinnamon sugar (reserving just a little to sprinkle). Place in a shallow baking dish and sprinkle remaining cinnamon sugar. Bake in oven for 15 minutes or until apples are nice and tender.

Baked Bananas

Recipe by Jodie McIver.

- *2 bananas*
- *2 tbs. honey*
- *1 tbs. melted butter*
- *¾ cup (80g) chopped nuts*

Preheat over to 180°C. Peel and halve the bananas and place onto a baking paper lined tray. Combine honey and butter together and drizzle over bananas. Bake for 10 minutes. Remove to serving plate and sprinkle with nuts.

Optional: Serve warm with ice cream.

Baked Marzipan

SERVES 4

- *125g marzipan, softened*
- *1 free range egg*
- *2 tbs. self raising flour, sifted*
- *1 ripe peach, thinly sliced*

Preheat oven to 160°C. Beat marzipan until soft, add egg and beat until well combined. Add flour and fold through. Dollop mixture evenly amongst small ramekins. Top with equal amounts of fanned out peach and bake for 20 minutes or until golden brown.

Optional: In the absence of fresh peaches, use pears, apples or any seasonal berries.

Caramelised Figs

MAKES 8

Light and Lovely!

- *8 fresh ripe figs, halved*
- *4 tbs. brown sugar*
- *200g Mascarpone cheese*
- *½ cup (60g) icing sugar*

Place fig halves on a baking paper lined tray. Sprinkle with sugar and grill them for 2–3 minutes, to lightly caramelise the sugar. Arrange the figs on a serving plate, and continue the cuts almost all the way down to the base, so the figs open like a flower. Beat mascarpone cheese with icing sugar. Divide the cheese among the figs and serve.

Chocolate Tofu Mousse

SERVES 4

This is heavenly.

- *350g pkt silken tofu (bought to room temperature)*
- *280g dark chocolate*
- *1 tbs. pure maple syrup*
- *1 tsp. vanilla extract*

Blend tofu in a food processor, blender, or with hand held mixer until just smooth. In a double boiler, melt chocolate over low heat. Stir constantly. Add maple syrup to melted chocolate and combine. Add to tofu with vanilla and mix until creamy. Pour into four small serving dishes. Chill until set.

Coconut Poached Pears

SERVES 4

- 400ml can coconut milk
- 2 tbs. organic raw sugar
- 1 cinnamon stick
- 4 small soft pears, peeled, cored and halved

Place the coconut milk, sugar and cinnamon in a saucepan over medium/low heat. Do not let the coconut milk boil or it will separate. Add the pears and cook for 15 minutes, turning once. Serve in bowls, with the warm coconut broth.

Figs in Vanilla Port

SERVES 4

- ¼ cup (50g) organic raw sugar
- ¾ cup (190ml) quality port
- 1 tsp. vanilla extract
- 8 fresh figs, halved

Place the sugar, port and vanilla in a non-stick frying pan over low heat and stir until the sugar has dissolved. Allow to simmer for 10 minutes or until syrupy. Place figs in serving bowls and pour the vanilla port over them.

Grilled Caramelised Pineapple

SERVES 4–6

- 1 large pineapple
- 2 tbs. (30ml) macadamia nut oil
- 2 tbs. brown sugar
- 1 lime

Peel pineapple. With a sharp knife, cut it crosswise into 2cm-thick slices. Brush the slices lightly with oil and grill for 7 minutes or until just browned. Turn slices over, brush with remaining oil and grill for 5–7 minutes longer. Immediately sprinkle pineapple with brown sugar. Cut into chunks and serve with lime wedges.

Grape Sorbet

SERVES 4

- 200g green grapes, frozen
- ½ tub sour cream
- ¼ cup (30g) icing sugar

Just before serving with coffee at the end of dinner, remove grapes from freezer, roll in sour cream to coat and then dust thoroughly with icing sugar.

Fig & Apple Compote

SERVES 6

- ½ cup (100g) brown sugar
- 1 lemon, sliced
- 6 baking apples
- 6 dried figs, chopped

Preheat oven to 180°C. Bring sugar and 1 cup (250ml) of water to a boil. Add lemon. Core apples, place in a baking dish and pop the figs into them. Pour lemon syrup over all and cover. Bake for 15–20 minutes, basting occasionally or until apples are tender and syrup thickened.

Frosted Lychees

SERVES 4

- 20 lychees, peeled and de-seeded

Place on a baking paper lined tray and freeze for at least 2 hours. Freezing these turns them into a mini-mouthful of a sorbet-like refreshment.

Fruit Kebabs

MAKES 4

- 2 kiwi, sliced in quarters
- 1 cup thick banana slices
- ½ cup seedless grapes
- 1 cup watermelon balls or cubes

Alternatively slide each of the above fruits onto a kebab.

Optional: Serve drizzled with honey or the delicious Berry Blast Sauce (see: Sauces, Salsas & Marinades).

Honey Custard

SERVES 2–4

- 3 tbs. cup honey
- 2 egg yolks
- 1 tbs. cornflour
- 1½ cups (375ml) milk

Combine honey, egg yolks and cornflour in a large bowl. Whisk until thick and creamy. Slowly whisk milk into egg yolk mixture before pouring the mixture into a small saucepan. Cook, whisking over a low heat, until custard thickens. Careful not to boil. Transfer into a bowl.

Hint: On cooling, custard tends to become thick, so stir in extra milk to desired consistency.

Kulfi

SERVES 4

One we learnt to make on a trip to England … It's now a favourite!

- 1.5 ltr. milk
- 3 tbs. raw organic sugar
- 3 cardamom pods
- ½ cup (50g) pistachio nuts, chopped

Pour the milk and sugar into a large, heavy saucepan. Bring to the boil, reduce heat and boil gently for 1 hour, stirring regularly. Place cardamom pods in a mortar and crush with a pestle. Add to milk and continue to boil until it has reduced and all that remains is about 2 cups. Grind nuts and stir into the milk. Pour into four 'kulfi' or popsicle moulds and freeze overnight.

Mango Dessert

SERVES 2

- 1 large mango
- 1 tbs. cinnamon sugar
- 1 lime, cut in half

Score the flesh on the mango cheeks into cubes. Sprinkle both with cinnamon sugar and pan fry or BBQ until golden. Transfer to a plate and drizzle with fresh lime juice. Garnish with lime wedges.

Melon Salad with Mint

SERVES 6

- 2 cups watermelon balls or cubes
- 2 cups rockmelon balls or cubes
- 2 cups honeydew balls or cubes
- 20 fresh mint leaves

Position fruit balls into a glass serving bowl, scatter with mint and gently toss.

Optional: For a little vigour, squeeze with fresh lime juice before serving.

Pineapple in Ginger Syrup

SERVES 4

- 1 fresh, ripe pineapple, peeled and chopped into chunks
- ⅓ cup (65g) organic raw sugar
- 1 knob of ginger, peeled and finely chopped
- 1 lemon, juiced

Place pineapple chunks into a heatproof bowl. Place sugar, ginger and 200ml water in a small saucepan and bring to a gentle simmer, stir until the sugar dissolves. Remove from heat and add lemon juice. Pour the syrup over the pineapple and leave to cool. Cover and chill until ready to serve.

Optional: Serve topped with some creamy yoghurt or ice cream.

Pineapple Creamy Tofu Dessert

SERVES 4

A recipe from Wendy Beattie.

- 200g soft silken tofu, whipped in a blender
- 1 cup diced, sweet, fresh pineapple
- 1 cup freshly grated coconut
- 2 tsp. vanilla

Combine all ingredients and chill in the refrigerator. Spoon into dessert dishes when ready to serve.

Optional: Garnish with freshly sliced kiwi fruit.

Pistachio & Rose Water Oranges

SERVES 4

- 4 oranges, peeled
- 2 tbs. (30ml) rose water
- 4 tbs. crushed pistachios
- 1 twig of fresh mint

Slice each orange into 6 rounds (reserve juice) and fan out on a serving plate. Mix juice and rose water and drizzle over oranges. Cover and chill for 30 minutes. Sprinkle with chopped pistachios to serve and garnish with a twig of mint.

Poached Oranges

SERVES 8

- 8 oranges
- ½ cup brown sugar
- ¼ cup dark rum, brandy or Grand Marnier

Strip the zest off four of the oranges using a zester. Peel the oranges, removing the pith as you go. Do this over a bowl to catch the orange juice. Cut each orange into three slices horizontally, then skewer with a toothpick so they keep their shape. Place in a large saucepan with the water, brown sugar and zest and simmer for 20 minutes. Carefully move the oranges to a serving dish. Add the alcohol to the cooking liquid, stir and pour over the oranges. Chill before serving.

Raspberry Tofu

SERVES 4

- *225g fresh raspberries*
- *350g soft silken tofu*
- *½ tsp. vanilla essence*
- *3 tbs. honey*

Combine all the ingredients and blend. Divide the mixture between four dessert dishes and chill for up to 2 hours. Garnish with reserved raspberries and serve.

Hint: Can use frozen raspberries, allow to thaw and drain before processing.

Raspberry & Lime Sorbet

SERVES 8

- *1 cup sugar*
- *500g fresh, ripe raspberries, washed*
- *1 lime, juiced*
- *1 twig of fresh mint leaves*

Heat 1 cup of water and sugar in a saucepan, bring to the boil stirring to dissolve. Boil for 5 minutes, then cool completely. Puree berries with lime juice and mint leaves in a blender and pour into a large bowl. Add the syrup and ⅔ cup (200ml) more water. Place in a paper lined loaf tin and put in the freezer. Remove every 15 minutes for the first hour and stir thoroughly, then let it freeze overnight. Slice to serve.

Roasted Peaches

SERVES 4

- 4 ripe peaches
- 1½ tsp. lemon juice
- 1 tbs. organic raw sugar

Preheat oven 200°C. Cut peaches in half and remove seeds. Toss the peach halves with lemon juice in a large bowl, add sugar and toss once again. Arrange halves cut-side up in a baking dish. Roast until the peaches are tender, 20–25 minutes. If the juices in the pan begin to burn, add a little water and cover the pan loosely with foil.

Optional: Serve with a small scoop of ice cream or some ricotta cheese drizzled with honey or nuts.

Stewed Apricots

SERVES 4

A recipe from the delightful Polly Davidson, Oxford UK.

- 250g plump, dried apricots
- 2½ cm (1 inch) piece of fresh ginger, grated
- 1 lemon

Pop the apricots into a saucepan and cover with water. Add ginger and zest of an entire lemon. Simmer contents for 20 minutes. Drain, reserving juice. Place apricots in a bowl and return juice to saucepan. Cook until it begins to caramelise. Pour the syrup over apricots and put in fridge. Yummy that day or the next.

Soufflé

MAKES 4

- *1 tbs. softened butter*
- *4 free range eggs, separated*
- *1 cup icing sugar (⅓ for ramekins)*
- *4 passionfruits*

Preheat oven to 180°C. Brush four 1 cup ramekins with butter to lightly grease. Sprinkle with a little icing sugar, shaking off any excess. In a bowl, cream the egg yolks with half the icing sugar until pale and the sugar has dissolved. Add the passionfruit pulp, mix and set aside. In a separate clean bowl, beat the egg whites. When you are halfway to peaks forming, gradually add the remaining sugar. Continue beating until firm peaks form (careful not to overbeat). Whisk some of the whites into the yolks then carefully fold through the remaining. Spoon the mixture into prepared ramekins and bake for 10–12 minutes or until soufflés are risen and slightly browned.

Optional: Passionfruits can be substituted for a myriad of ingredients, chocolate, coconut, lemon, raspberry, crushed pineapple to name a few.

Tea Scented Mandarins

SERVES 4

- *4 mandarins, peeled and segmented*
- *½ cup hot black tea*
- *2 tbs. honey*
- *Pinch of ground cardamom*

Place mandarins in a small bowl. Pour tea over them and drizzle with honey and sprinkle with cardamom. Allow to sit for 10 minutes before serving.

Warm Bananas with Dates & Cardamom

SERVES 2–4

- 2 tbs. ghee
- 2 bananas, sliced in half
- ⅛ tsp. cardamom
- 12 dates, chopped

Place ghee in a frying pan over medium heat and add bananas. Cook for 2–3 minutes or until caramelised. Remove, set aside and in the frying pan add dates and cardamom with ¼ cup water. Simmer until dates are nice and soft. Place bananas on a serving plate and drizzle with sauce.

Watermelon with Lemon Cheese

SERVES 8

- 2kg watermelon, peeled and chopped into cubes
- 250g ricotta cheese
- 1 lemon, zest and juice
- 2 tbs. icing sugar

Place the watermelon in a covered bowl in the refrigerator. Mix the ricotta cheese with the rind and juice of ½ a lemon in a bowl and beat with a fork. Add icing sugar to taste and more lemon juice if necessary. A sharp, lemon taste marries with the subtleness of watermelon beautifully. Serve the chilled watermelon in bowls with spoonfuls of lemon cheese on top.

The Meanest Mother

Written by Bobbi Pingaro

I had the meanest mother in the world.

While other kids had lollies for breakfast, I had to eat egg, cereal and toast. While other kids had cans of drink and chips for lunch, I had to have a sandwich. As you can guess, my dinner was not only different from the other kids, I had to eat it at a table and not in front of the television set.

My mother also insisted on knowing where we were at all times. You'd think we were on a chain gang or something. She had to know who our friends were, where we were going and she even told us when we had to be home.

I'm ashamed to admit it, but my mother actually had the nerve to break child labour laws. She made us wash the dishes, make our own beds and even learn to cook. That woman must have stayed awake at night, just thinking up things for us kids to do!

By the time we were teenagers our whole life became even more unbearable. Our old fashioned mother refused to let us date until we were 15 and then insisted that boys had to come to the door to collect girls from our family, instead of tooting the car horn for us to come running.

She really raised a bunch of squares. None of us kids were ever arrested for stealing or busted for dope.

And who do we thank for this? You're right, OUR MEAN MOTHER. Every day we hear cries from our people and politicians about what our country really needs.

What our country really needs is ...

MORE MEAN MOTHERS JUST LIKE MINE!

For The Children

*A dream is only a dream without courage and determination
to make it real!*

Anonymous

Apple Oatmeal

SERVES 2

- *1 cup rolled oats*
- *½ cup stewed apples (or applesauce)*
- *½ tsp. cinnamon*
- *2 tbs. brown sugar*

Pour 2 cups water, oats, and a pinch of salt into a medium-size pot on
the stove. Heat the mixture until it boils, then reduce heat. Using a
wooden spoon, stir in the apples and cinnamon. Continue to stir for
5 minutes. Pour the oatmeal into two bowls and sprinkle with brown
sugar. Allow to cool for a couple of minutes before serving.

Apple Purée

SERVES 2

- *2 apples, pared and cored*
- *¼ cup (62ml) apple juice*
- *3 cinnamon sticks*
- *2 tbs. honey*

Place all ingredients in saucepan and bring to a boil. Reduce heat and
simmer until apples are soft. Remove from heat, take out cinnamon
sticks and let cool. Place in blender or food processor and process
until smooth.

Banana Tofu Smoothie

SERVES 1

- ⅓ cup (85ml) apple juice
- 125g silken tofu, drained
- 1 banana
- 125g honey flavoured yoghurt

Place all ingredients in a blender with 4 cubes of ice and blend.

Chicken Curry

SERVES 2

- ½ cup natural yoghurt
- 1½ tsp. coriander
- 1½ tsp. curry powder
- 2 x 120g free range chicken breasts

Preheat oven 180°C. Combine yoghurt, coriander and curry powder in a shallow bowl. Add chicken to yoghurt sauce and coat evenly. Place chicken in a greased casserole dish. Spoon remainder of yoghurt sauce on top and bake for 35 minutes or until cooked.

Chocolate-Kissed Strawberries

SERVES 2

- *80g dark chocolate*
- *1 punnet strawberries*

Rinse fruit well. Do not remove stems. Blot dry with a paper towel and set aside. Melt chocolate in the top of a double boiler, stirring constantly. When chocolate has melted, remove top portion of the double boiler. To coat strawberries, hold one at a time by the top and dip into chocolate. Coat completely except for stem area. Let cool.

Hint: The redder the strawberry is closer to the hull, the sweeter.

Creamy Rice Pudding

SERVES 4–6

A recipe from Wendy Beattie and it is yummy!

- *½ cup (100g) organic raw sugar*
- *1.5 ltr. milk*
- *1 cup (185g) arborio rice*
- *1 lemon, finely zested*

Preheat oven 180°C. Place sugar, milk, rice, and zest with a pinch of salt into a baking dish, stir well. Cover dish with foil, place in the oven under the quince and bake for 1¾ hours or until thick and creamy.

Optional: Add ½ tsp. of cinnamon to the mix prior to baking.

Crepes

MAKES 10

Recipe from Mia Burnie.

- *1 cup (175g) plain flour*
- *1 free range egg, beaten*
- *1 cup (250ml) milk*
- *2 tbs. (30g) butter*

Sift flour and mix with egg. Gradually add milk and ½ cup of water. Then add a pinch of salt. Into a small non-stick frying pan, melt a little butter. Use ¼ cup of mixture for each crepe. Cook on one side for 2 minutes or until it starts to bubble, flip and cook for a further minute.

Optional: Serve with sliced bananas and a sprinkling of cinnamon or nutmeg.

Grape Popsicles

- *1 bunch white grapes*
- *1 bunch purple grapes*

Remove from stems and freeze. These frozen grapes are healthy little treats on really hot days.

Optional: Another fruit to try is blueberries – Jaxson's favourite frozen summer treat!

Fish Cakes

SERVES 4–6

- *1kg potatoes, peeled and chopped*
- *1 onion, diced*
- *415g can salmon*
- *¼ cup chopped parsley*

Boil and mash potatoes. Add onion, salmon, parsley, salt and pepper and mix together well. It is easier to mix this together if you do it when the potato is still hot. Chill for 1-2 hours. Shape into patties, pop into a non-stick frying pan and over medium heat, cook for 4 minutes each side or until golden brown.

Frozen Yoghurt Ices

MAKES 2

- *250g yoghurt*
- *1 tbs. honey*

Mix honey into yoghurt. If you don't have ice cream moulds, pour yoghurt into paper cups and fill them almost to the top. Stretch a small piece of plastic wrap across the top of each cup. Using a popsicle stick, poke a hole in the plastic wrap. Stand the stick straight up in the centre of the cup. Put the cups in the freezer until the yoghurt is frozen solid. Remove the plastic wrap, peel away the paper cup and eat.

Homemade Peanut Butter

MAKES 1 CUP

- *1½ cup unsalted roasted peanuts*
- *1 tbs. peanut oil*

Mix the peanuts with the peanut oil, and pour the mixture into the food processor. Process the mixture until it's very smooth. Store in a sealed container in the fridge. It will be fine for up to 2 weeks.

Optional: for Chunky Peanut Butter: Take ¼ cup out of your 1½ cups of peanuts and set them aside. Proceed as above, when mixture is smooth, then stir in the peanuts that you had set aside. Process a few seconds more to create the chunks in your chunky peanut butter.

Hummus

MAKES 1 CUP

- *400g can chickpeas, drained, liquid reserved*
- *1 clove garlic, crushed*
- *2 tsp. ground cumin*
- *1 tbs. (15ml) olive oil*

In a blender or food processor combine all ingredients with ½ tsp. salt. Blend on low speed, gradually adding reserved bean liquid, until desired consistency is achieved.

Polenta Crusted Fish Fingers

SERVES 4

- *2 pieces of firm white fish, cut into fingers*
- *1 cup polenta*
- *¼ cup parmesan, grated*
- *2 free range egg whites, beaten*

Combine polenta and parmesan, dip fish into egg whites then into the polenta mixture and coat well. Set in the fridge for 10 minutes then pan fry and serve with a dipping sauce.

Optional: Great as a finger food for kids.

Rice Pilaf

- *2 tbs. (30g) butter*
- *3 cloves garlic, crushed*
- *1 cup (185g) long grain rice, rinsed*
- *2 cups (500ml) vegetable stock*

In a non-stick frying pan melt butter. Add garlic and rice and cook for 3 minutes, stirring continuosly until the rice turns opaque. Add stock and reduce heat, cover and simmer for 20–25 minutes or until liquid is absorbed and rice is tender.

Optional: Add some onion with the garlic and rice. Stir in coriander to serve.

Rockmelon Sorbet

SERVES 8

- 1 kg ripe rockmelon
- 1 cup (220g) caster sugar
- 1 cup (250ml) water
- ½ lemon, zest and juice

Chop melon coarsely. Place on a baking tray and into the freezer until frozen. Over medium heat, combine sugar and water in small saucepan. Bring to a boil, stirring then simmer for 5 minutes or until slightly thickened, remove from heat, cool and refrigerate until required. Fifteen minutes before making sorbet, remove the melon from freezer and place it and the sugar syrup into a blender and process until smooth. Add lemon zest and juice to taste.
Stir and pour into a freezer container, seal and refreeze.

Sausage Rolls

MAKES 16

Recipe from the lovely Cathy Morrison.

- 400g free range chicken mince
- 1 carrot, peeled and grated
- 2 tbs. honey
- 2 sheets butter puff pastry

Preheat oven 200°C. Mix together mince, carrot and honey and season. Lay a sheet of pastry on a flat surface. Cut sheet in half. Spoon mince mixture down the centre of each pastry half. Fold pastry over filling, overlapping the edges and placing the join underneath, to enclose. Cut each into 4 short pieces. Place on a baking paper lined tray. Repeat with remaining pastry and filling. Bake for 30 minutes or until golden.

Stuffed Tomatoes

SERVES 4

Recipe from Melinda Dines, her son Harrison 9 looooves these!

- *4 medium tomatoes*
- *2 hard boiled eggs, chopped*
- *1 (200g) potato, peeled and cooked*
- *½ cup peas, cooked*

Preheat oven to 150°C. Cut the top off each tomato and carefully scoop out the pulp. In a medium bowl, mash the eggs and potato, gently fold in tomato pulp, peas and season to taste. Scoop back into the tomato shells. Place each on an oven tray and bake for 10–15 minutes or until hot.

Teriyaki Chicken

SERVES 2

- *2 free range chicken thighs, cut into bite size pieces*
- *½ cup (125ml) mirin*
- *2 tbs. (30ml) soy sauce*
- *1 tsp. brown sugar*

Mix together mirin, soy sauce and brown sugar. In a non stick frying pan on medium heat, add 1 tbs. water and cook the chicken. Add the sauce and bring to the boil, lower heat and boil gently until the sauce thickens and caramelises.

Optional: Serve over rice with some steamed broccoli.

Drinks

Apple Juice

SERVES 1

- *1 large apple*
- *1 tbs. honey*

Core the apples, cut into quarters and juice. Stir through honey and serve over crushed ice.

Apple & Kiwi Juice

MAKES 1

- *2 apples*
- *3 kiwi fruit, peeled*

Cut the fruit into small pieces and then juice. Stir, pour into a tall glass over crushed ice and enjoy.

Tip: Studies have shown that consuming 2 or 3 kiwi fruit each day can help thin the blood and possibly take the place of a daily aspirin.

Banana & Vanilla Smoothie

MAKES 2

- 2 large ripe bananas, frozen
- 1 cup milk
- ¾ cup vanilla yoghurt
- 4 tbs. LSA mix

Blend all ingredients together and serve.

Cardamom Tea

SERVES 4–6

- 2 tbs. black tea
- 6 cardamom pods
- 5cm piece of cinnamon

Place all ingredients in a tea pot and pour in 5 cups of boiling water (6 if you like your tea on the weaker side) let the tea steep for 4 minutes. Serve this with milk and sugar, honey and lemon, or as is.

Detox Juice

SERVES 1

Recipe from the inspirational Doreen Virtue.

- *1cm ginger root*
- *2 apples*
- *2 lemons*

This is a great detoxifying drink to jump-start your morning. Peel the skin of the ginger root. Slice apples into 4 equal parts and remove the core. Remove the skin and rind from the lemons. Juice the lemons and one slice of apple and add the ginger, then the rest of the apple slices. Works wonders before breakfast.

Double Strawberry Shake

SERVES 1

This makes a wonderfully thick shake.

- *¾ cup frozen strawberry yoghurt*
- *¾ cup freshly chopped strawberries*
- *¼ cup (62ml) soy milk*

In a blender, combine all of the ingredients with 4 cubes of ice and blend until thick and smooth. Pour into glass and serve.

Hint: If you like it a bit more liquid, increase the soymilk to ⅓ cup or ½ cup as desired.

Ginger Tea

SERVES 4

- 4cm piece of fresh ginger root
- 4 cups water
- 1 tsp. honey
- 1 lemon slice

Peel the ginger root and slice it into thin slices. Bring the water to a boil in a saucepan. Add ginger. Cover and reduce to a simmer for 15–20 minutes. Strain the tea. Add honey and lemon to taste. Bring to the boil.

Tip: Ginger tea has a spicy, invigorating taste. It's used as a home remedy for indigestion, nausea, and to ward off colds, flu, and sore throats.

Ginger, Lemon & Honey Tea

SERVES 1

- ½ cm fresh ginger
- ¼ lemon, juiced
- 1 tsp. honey

Crush ginger before adding to 1 cup boiling water. Allow to sit for 1 minute. Add juice and honey, stir well and enjoy.

Iced Lemon Tea

MAKES 2

- 4 premium blend tea bags
- 4 tsp. honey
- 1 lemon
- Mint to garnish

Make 1 cup of tea using all the teabags. Infuse for 4 minutes, remove bags and allow to cool. Pour tea into a large jug and add honey and 4 tsp. lemon juice and stir to dissolve. Pour over 2 cups cool water, chill in the fridge. Serve in a tall glass with ice cubes and garnished with a slice of lemon and a twig of fresh mint.

Mango & Mint Smoothie

MAKES 2

- 2 large ripe mangoes
- 400g can coconut milk
- ¾ cup yoghurt
- 6 large mint leaves

Blend all ingredients together with several cubes of ice and serve.

Moroccan Mint Tea

MAKES 2

- 2 tsp. mint
- 2 tsp. green tea
- 2 tsp. honey

Pop all ingredients into a tea pot with 2 cups of boiling water.

Prune Juice

MAKES 2 CUPS

- *125g prunes, depitted*
- *2 ½ cups water*

Simmer prunes for 30 minutes so that the water is lightly trembling. Remove from heat and allow to cool before pureeing in a blender.

Tip: Simmer a mixture of 5 parts water to 1 part prunes for the quantity you desire.

Watermelon Juice

MAKES 2

- *½ watermelon, seeds removed*
- *3 tsp. palm sugar*
- *¼ lemon, juiced*

Juice watermelon in a blender. Add palm sugar and a few drops of lemon juice. Blend and serve in a tall glass over ice.

Handy Hints & Tips

The past is history, the future a mystery, and the present is a gift.

A Very Wise Man

Antiseptic: Cinnamon is known as one of nature's strongest antiseptics. It also contains sedative components and is believed to lower blood-sugar levels.

Arthritis: Lemons are a useful remedy for arthritis and vitamin C deficiency.

Asthma: Lemons are useful remedy for asthma, very beneficial taken in the morning squeezing 2 tbs. fresh lemon juice into a glass of warm water.

Bad Breath: The aromatic flavour in cardamom seeds sweetens the breath and has a coolness similar to mint. Chewing some cardamom seeds is an effective breath freshener or after dinner palate cleanser.

Challenges: Whenever you are feeling challenged, remember what Louise L. Hay always says: "All is well, you are safe."

Chilli: The health benefits of eating chillies are well documented but suprisingly little known, despite the many numerous and profound ways in which they are known to aid, relieve and prevent many conditions.

Cleaning Agents: Lemons are acidic and can provide some antibacterial and antiseptic properties for cleaning. Vinegar is cost effective and an excellent environment friendly cleanser. Use it in a spray bottle and spray into your basins, shower and toilet. Allow to sit for a few hours to kill bacteria before wiping over to keep the areas clean.

Cleanser: Lemons are very powerful and a natural cleanser keeping our stomach, liver and intestines in good shape ... *Right, warm water and freshly squeezed lemon juice all round!*

Clear Nasal Passage: Due to its antispasmodic properties, basil can be used to ease an upset stomach and stimulate the cilia in the nose to help clear the nasal passages.

Colds, Coughs and Sniffles: Nothing beats 1 tbs. honey mixed with ½ tsp. ginger and a squirt of lemon juice all stirred in a mug of warm water.

Concentration: Nutmeg is said to increase concentration ... *Right, where's the nutmeg?*

Constipation: Pears and prunes are both really beneficial in the treatment of constipation.

Coriander: Coriander is used to aid in digestion. It is also known to alleviate migraine headaches.

Decluttering: Albert Einstein said "Out of clutter comes simplicity and in the middle of difficulty, lies and opportunity."

Depression: Drink tea with ¼ tsp. of powdered cardamom seeds. You can also try crushing cloves and adding to sage, and adding some ginseng powder to camomile or peppermint tea to lift mild depression.

Diarrhea: Marjoram and nutmeg both promote digestion and help relieve diarrhea.

Digestion & Circulation: Cayenne pepper is used to stimulate the digestive and circulatory systems. Parsley too strengthens the digestive system and is also used as a diuretic.

Dill: Helps to calm a nervous stomach. It is also known to kill intestinal bacteria.

Disinfectant: Cloves are known for their disinfectant properties. Also used to treat toothaches and reduce inflammation.

Energy Booster & Immune Builder: The three key health benefits of honey is that it is nature's energy booster, a great immunity system builder and a natural remedy for certain ailments. Honey's antioxidant and anti–bacterial properties can help improve the digestive system and help you stay healthy and fight disease.

Gas, flatulence or wind: Chop up 2cm of ginger and add to 1 cup of warm water. Drink before you step into an elevator or small crowded area !!!!

Ginger: Ginger helps to stimulate the heart and circulatory system and is also know for its ability to reduce inflammation.

Gout: Lemons are a useful remedy for gout and urine retention.

Fatigue: Saffron eases fatigue and exhaustion, it also strengthens the heart and nervous system.

Head Lice: The acetic acid in the vinegar helps kill off the eggs. Before applying shampoo to your hair, massage your hair with the vinegar and a few drops of tea tree oil. This will help get rid of the adult lice and the nymphs. Another home remedy for head lice is massaging the head with mayonnaise. Remember you will still need to comb out all the eggs, the oil in mayonnaise helps achieve this easily. Most egg lice will be found around the ears and nape of the head.

Health benefits of grapefruit: Are enormous. A glass of chilled grapefruit juice, especially in winter, will increase your vitamin C intake. Grapefruit is full with the benefits of nutrients, vitamins, potassium, lycopene and refrigerant. Along with these, it also contains calcium, sugar and phosphorous.

Healthy eyes: Juice a carrot and mix it with a teaspoon of honey. Works wonders if you have it before breakfast.

Heartburn: Cardamom is a member of the ginger family and is used to relieve stomach problems and heartburn.

Heart disease, stroke and hypertension: Garlic is thought to prevent all, it is quite simply a nutritional powerhouse.

Herbs for pest control: Across the board, herbs seem to be useful reducing garden bugs. Sage for example, will deter carrot flies and cabbage moths. Chives are generally helpful and when snipped for use, the strong odour provides a deterrent. Basil deters bugs from tomatoes. Rosemary has an oil that repels mosquitoes. Within the vegetable garden, a mixture of vegetable and herbs will give you twice the protection.

Inflammation of the mouth and throat: Lemons help heal hoarseness, inflammation and digestive disorders.

Insomnia: Lemons are a useful remedy for nervousness, insomnia and heart palpitations.

Lemons as a cleaning agent: Are acidic and can provide some antibacterial and antiseptic properties for cleaning.

Louis Diat says: "There are five elements: Earth, air, fire, water & *garlic.*"

Lower blood pressure: Chives are used to promote good digestion and to help to lower high blood pressure. They also make a good diuretic.

Maple syrup: is one of the few unprocessed good sugars that provide micronutrients as well as calories to the body. It is high in minerals including zinc and manganese.

Menstrual cramps: If you experience menstrual cramps, drink a lot of warm liquids. This helps exude warmth to your muscles and relaxes them.

Mucus: Marjoram loosens mucus to aid in the recovery of bronchitis.

Natural insect repellent: Basil when planted is often used as a natural insect repellent.

Onion: Recently onions were found to raise the HDL cholesterol, which helps to clear the fatty deposits from the arteries.

Orange: The orange is one of the best sources of the powerful antioxidant vitamin C, and has multiple health benefits.

Oregano: Oregano is used for indigestion, flatulence, bloating and to help ease stomach pains. Stand 3 tbs. freshly crushed oregano leaves in 1 cup of boiling water for 10 minutes.

Parsley: Parsley is the world's most popular herb and is loaded with goodness. It helps strengthens the digestive system and is also used as a diuretic. It also has high levels of Vitamin C among other health benefits.

Pepper: Stimulates the taste-buds causing reflex stimulation of gastric secretions, improving digestion and treating gastro-intestinal upsets and flatulence. Pepper calms nausea and raises body temperature, making it valuable for treating fevers and chills.

Peppermint: This can be used to treat morning sickness and motion sickness. A daily cup of peppermint tea is said to work wonders for calm as it helps fight stress!

Premenstrual Syndrome: Draw a luxurious hot water bath. This will relax and relieve all the tired muscles in your body. Turn off the lights, take the phone off the hook and put a 'Do not disturb' sign on the door and sip on a mug of camomile tea.

Promoting good blood flow: Horseradish inhibits the growth of bacteria and viruses and helps promote good blood flow.

Respiratory Congestion: Anise is used to loosen mucus and clear respiratory congestion. Also used to relieve bloating and indigestion.

Saffron: Eases fatigue and exhaustion and also strengthens the heart and nervous system.

Salt: Has been used since the beginning of recorded history as a preservative and flavour enhancer. Prior to the discovery of various chemicals, salt served the purpose of many modern chemicals. It has been used as a cleaning agent and medical disinfectant.

Sore throats: Thyme relaxes cramps and gas and also helps to relieve sore throats.

Stimulates the cardiovascular system: Nutmeg helps stimulates the cardiovascular system.

Stomach Ailments: Allspice has a clove like taste and can be used to treat stomach ailments. Dried ginger can be used for stomach problems such as stomach-ache, diarrhea and nausea.

Strengthen immune system: Coconuts are seen by some as a miracle food, helping to protect and cure the body of internal and external ailments. Coconut milk has many uses, most of which build up the immune system and the body's defences. To take advantage of the health benefits, find coconut milk in the ethnic foods section of a local grocery store or make it at home.

Stress: The leaves of basil have been found beneficial in the treatment of stress. They are regarded as an anti-stress agent and recent studies suggest that even healthy persons should chew 12 basil leaves twice a day, morning and evening, for preventing stress. The herb sage is also considered valuable in combatting stress. A tea prepared from the leaves of this plant should be given in the treatment of this condition. Pour a cup of boiling water over one teaspoon of dried sage leaves, cover and allow time to infuse. Strain and sweetened naturally with honey, if desired. In the case of fresh leaves, a tablespoon of coarsely chopped sage leaves should be used and tea prepared in the same way.

Success: As Winston Churchill said: "Success is going from one challenge to another without loss of enthusiasm."

Sunburn: This one is almost worth eating! Get some fresh yoghurt, mix in some barley and turmeric in equal proportions and then apply it on the sunburn to provide relief.

Sunburn, Skin Allergies & Injuries: Aloe Vera is highly recommended for healing purposes and you can use it internally as well as externally. One of the key benefits of Aloe Vera is in the treatment of bruises and burns. It is particularly beneficial for skin allerries and skin injuries. Herbal medication specialists use it for the treatment of ulcers, skin burns and even to counter the effect of poison.

Tarragon: Stimulates the appetite and also relieves gas.

Thomas Jefferson said: "I've seldom regretted eating too little."

Toothache: Cloves are used to treat toothaches and reduce inflammation.

Turmeric: This can be used to reduce the risk of gallstones and is also an anti-inflammatory.

Warts: The milky juice of fresh figs is a valuable remedy. This juice should be extracted from the fresh, barely-ripe fruits and applied on the warts several times a day. The treatment should be continued for two weeks.

Bibliography

Books

Cyndi O'Meara, **Changing Habits Changing Lives**. Penguin Books Victoria, Australia, 2000.

Laurent & Chantal Vancam, **Chef Laurent Caters for Kids**, Firefly Press, Buderim, Australia, 2009.

Lowery, Barbara. **Quick & Easy Cookbook**. 176 South Creek Road, Dee Why West, Australia. Summit Books, 1977.

Deepak Chopra. **Seven Spiritual Laws of Success**.

Maya Tiwari. **Ayurveda – A Life of Balance: The Complete Guide to Ayurvedic Nutrition & Body Types with Recipes**.

Vasant D. Lad & Angela Werneke **Ayurveda: Science of Self-Healing: A Practical Guide.**

Bart van Olphen & Tom Kime, **Fish Tales**. Kyle Cathie Limited, Great Britain, 2009

Christine Ingram **The Cooks Guide to Vegetables**. Anness Publishing Limited, 1996

The Encyclopedia of Cooking a practical guide. Rebo Productions Ltd, 1997

Dr Jenny Brand-Miller, Kaye Foster-Powell, and Joanna McMillan-Price. **Glycemic Index Cooking made easy**. Rodale Inc USA 2007

Oneka Lai **Popular Rice Dishes**. Australian Universities Press, 1973

Laura L.Ulrich. **Good Food How to Prepare It**. Signs Publishing Company, Victoria Australia, 1912

Ruth Berolzheimer. **Culinary Arts Institute Encyclopedic Cookbook**. Culinary Arts Institute, Chicago USA, 1910

Fish cooking made easy. Marshall Cavendish Books Limited, 1979

Cook Vegetarian Magazine. Maze Media Ltd, Colchester England, 2000

Australian Women's Health Magazine. Pacific Mags, NSW, 2010

Australian Healthy Food Guide. Healthy Life Media Pty Ltd, NSW, 2009

Weight Watchers Magazine. Self published 2010

Woolworths Australian Good Taste. News Magazines Pty, NSW, 2010

Coles Health & Beauty Magazine: December 2009, March 2010. Coles.

Cook Vegetarian Magazine: March 2010 & April 2010. Maze Media Ltd, Colchester England, 2000

Australian Women's Health Magazine. Pacific Magazines, Level 4, 139 Murray Street, Pyrmont, NSW 2009.

Australian Healthy Food Guide: October & November 2009, February, March & April 2010. Healthy Life Media Pty Ltd, NSW.

Weight Watchers Magazine: February, March & April 2010 Editions. Weight Watchers.

Woolworths Australian Good Taste: March, April & May 2010 Editions. News Magazines Ltd Pty, NSW.

Webpages

Nourishing Body and Soul, the Chopra Center Cookbook, Deepak Chopra, M.D, David Simon, M.D & Leanne Backer
http://store.chopra.com/productinfo.asp?item=61

The Biggest Home Remedies Guide
http://www.ayurvediccure.com/homeremedies.htm

Some of the Best Insect Repellents are Herbal Repellents
www.herbalinsectrepellant.com/

Recipes for the Whole Family
http://kidshealth.org/parent/recipes/index.html

Top 10 Superfoods & Their Benefits
http://www.squidoo.com/top_10_superfoods

Bouquet Garni Definition
http://www.culinaryschmooze.com/chef-recipes/french/seasonings-spices/bouquet-garni-definition/

How to Cook Fish
http://www.deliaonline.com/how-to-cook/fish-and-shellfish/how-to-cook-fish.html

The secrets of Eating Well
http://wellness.glam.com/photos/slideshow/secrets_of_eating_well/

The Best Herbs for Optimal Health
http://vitamins-minerals.suite101.com/article.cfm/the_best_herbs_for_optimal_health

Gourmet Garden Herbs and Spices
http://www.gourmetgarden.com/au/

Spice of Life: Health Benefits of Spices and Herbs
http://www.fitnessmagazine.com/recipes/healthy-eating/nutrition/health-benefits-of-spices-herbs/

The Best Home Remedies
http://www.best-home-remedies.com

Article Base
http://www.articlesbase.com/

All Ayurveda
http://www.allayurveda.com/herbalcure5.asp

Home Remedies for You
http://www.home-remedies-for-you.com/remedy/Head-Lice.html

Goodness of Mangoes
http://www.natural-homeremedies.org/blog/goodness-of-mango-2/

Recipes for Kids
http://kidshealth.org/kid/recipes/index.html

Raisins
http://flavoursofindia.tripod.com/raisins.html

EHow, How to do Just About Anything
http://www.ehow.com/how

Food Facts
http://www.vegsoc.org/cordonvert/recipes/celeria.html

5 Easy Ways to Cook Fish
http://www.heb.com/mealtime/CT-easyFish.jsp

Homemade Pasta Dough
http://www.italiansrus.com/recipes/pastadough.htm

Biographies

Kim McCosker

Kim was born in Stanthorpe and raised in Mundubbera. Schooled on the Gold Coast, completing a Bachelor of International Finance, Kim trained with MLC as a Financial Planner completing her Diploma in Financial Planning through Deakin University. Kim's natural ease with people, her ability to communicate effortlessly and her relaxed confidence served her well as a successful financial adviser and later as the Queensland State Manager of MLC Private Client Services. Kim worked for seven years in the finance industry before finally resigning to spend the time raising her beautiful boys.

It was during this phase of her life that *4 Ingredients* was born. Kim had the idea for some time, but it was at the suggestion of her lifelong friend Rachael Bermingham they write it. Taking a year to compile and cook, *4 Ingredients* (or Kim's fourth child as she lovingly refers to it) was born in March, 2007. From an initial print run of 2,000 that were *'never going to sell'* Kim and Rachael went onto orchestrate what the trade now refers to as *'An absolute phenomenon!'* They have now sold over 3 million copies of their titles, filmed two TV series for the Lifestyle Channel (broadcast into 12 countries worldwide), produced an iTunes App called 4 Ingredients, are working on a fabulous version for the Apple iPad, launched a unique cookware range and are developing a debut supermarket line. The future is very exciting and when asked about it, Kim happily shares *'The aim is to continue building a dynamic enterprise that not only we, but Australia is very proud of.'*

But of all that has been accomplished, the most rewarding by far has been the birth of her three precious boys Morgan 8, Hamilton 5 and Flynn 2. For Kim, family is *the most important thing in the world* and with the loving support of her wonderful husband Glen, she is able to juggle the demands of a busy work life around her treasured home life. Life presents many opportunities, but having the courage and the time to pursue them in what is an ever increasingly busy and demanding world is hard. But Kim is living proof that you can achieve whatever you want in life with a *great idea* and *lots of HARD WORK!*

You can contact Kim by:

E   info@4ingredients.com.au
O   (07) 5341 8282

Rachael Bermingham

RACHAEL THE MUM: is an energetic, dynamic and proud work from home mum to three gorgeous little boys; Jaxson 5, newborn and twins Bowie & Casey.

RACHAEL THE ADVENTURER: Rachael Bermingham (nee Moore) was born in Stanthorpe on Queensland's Darling Downs. Always seeking adventure, Rachael trained to become one of three women in Australia to professionally feed sharks at Underwater World which she did for three years, was a state champion in martial arts, and even did a small stint as a stuntwoman at Warner Brothers Movie World.

RACHAEL THE AUTHOR: Rachael has written five bestselling books in the last four years and is regarded as the #1 female self-published author in Australia. Rachael co-wrote, self-published and self-funded her first book *Read My Lips* in 2005 (a motivational book for women on how to achieve their goals) while breastfeeding her son Jaxson before being asked to utilise her book writing experience and marketing talent to write what has become the phenomenally successful 4 Ingredients cookbook series with Kim McCosker. Rachael released her fifth and first solo title *How to Write Your Own Book and Make it a Bestseller* which also became an overnight bestseller.

RACHAEL THE BUSINESS WOMAN: A natural entrepreneur, Rachael's talent for business shone early on when she succeeded in opening her first business at the tender age of 19 (a hair salon). In her twenty years in business she has become most renowned for her ability and natural flair in building multi-million dollar companies from a home base around family commitments with clever 'no cost' marketing and business tactics coupled with effective time management and goal setting strategies. Her passion for helping others to succeed and transform their goals into achievements eventually evolved in the form of authoring books and becoming an entertaining, and inspiring motivational speaker, role model, trainer and mentor to women in six different countries.

RACHAEL AT HOME: When Rachael's not working on new books, whipping up something fabulous in the kitchen, speaking up a storm on stage, or working on or marketing her four different business interests she can be found enjoying what she loves most; 'chillaxing' at home her fabulous family and friends soaking up the spectacular sun, surf and sand of the beautiful Sunshine Coast.

You can contact Rachael by:

E   rachael@4ingredients.com.au
O   0488 480 006

About Deepak Chopra M.D.

Deepak Chopra is a world-renowned leader in the fields of holistic health and human potential. He is a *New York Times* bestselling author of *The Seven Spiritual Laws of Success*, and numerous books and audio programs that cover every aspect of mind, body, and spirit. His books have been translated into more than fifty languages, and he travels widely throughout the world promoting peace, health and wellbeing.

Index

Potato & Rice 114

Vegetables 123

MAINS 139

Poultry 139

The Meanest Mother...221

FOR THE CHILDREN...222

DRINKS...231

Handy Hints & Tips 237

Bibliography 242

Biographies 245

Invitation

To all who contributed a recipe to this book, by way of email, post or phone, we would like to extend *a sincere* thank you.

IF YOU have a fabulous 4 or 5 ingredient recipe and think that others would enjoy cooking it, please submit it at **www.4ingredients.com.au**

Be sure to include your name, suburb or town for acknowledgment.

Thank You

Best Wishes & Happy Cooking!

Rachael & Kim

www.4ingredients.com.au

We hope you enjoyed this Hay House book. If you'd like to
receive our online catalogue featuring additional information on
Hay House books and products, or if you'd like to
find out more about the Hay Foundation, please contact:

Hay House Australia Pty. Ltd.,
18/36 Ralph St., Alexandria NSW 2015
Phone: +61 2 9669 4299 • Fax: +61 2 9669 4144
www.hayhouse.com.au

HEAD OFFICE (USA)
Hay House, Inc.,
P.O. Box 5100, Carlsbad, CA 92018-5100
Phone: (760) 431 7695 • Fax: (760) 431 6948
www.hayhouse.com®

INTERNATIONAL
Hay House UK, Ltd.,
292B Kensal Rd., London W10 5BE
Phone: 44 20 8962 1230 • Fax: 44 20 8962 1239
www.hayhouse.co.uk

Hay House South Africa Pty. Ltd.,
P.O. Box 990, Witkoppen 2068
Phone/Fax: 27 11 467 8904
www.hayhouse.co.za

Hay House Publishers India.,
Muskaan Complex, Plot No. 3, B-2, Vasant Kunj,
New Delhi 110 070
Phone: 91 11 4176 1620 • Fax: 91 11 41761630
www.hayhouse.co.in

Tune in to HayHouseRadio.com® for the best in inspirational talk radio
featuring top Hay House authors! And, sign up via the Hay House Australia
website to receive the Hay House online newsletter and stay informed about
what's going on with your favourite authors. You'll receive announcements about
Discounts and Offers, Special Events, Product Highlights, Giveaways and more!
www.hayhouse.com.au